HEALING AND WHOLENESS

by R. Eugene Sterner

**Published by
Warner Press, Inc.
Anderson, Indiana**

TABLE OF CONTENTS

Introduction

HEALING is a normal part of the ministry of the Church. It belongs in the relationship of Christian believers who "bear one another's burdens and thus fulfill the law of Christ." The New Testament recognizes the Holy Spirit's gifts of faith, of healing, and of miracles along with other gifts. Healing has attended the ministry of the Church in its finest and most vital times. It has, by and large, attended the ministry committed to the validity and authenticity of the Scriptures as the inspired word of God. Jesus linked preaching the gospel of the Kingdom with the ministry of healing. Nothing more demonstrated Jesus' divine power nor expressed God's great love for human beings than the healing of bodies. And nothing gained the attention and confidence of people so much as healing.

In many churches this ministry has been neglected. It seems to be regarded as something limited to the first century church. But all across the years there have been experiences of healing. Clearly it is taught in the Scriptures.

There is need for fresh, serious attention to this subject. Our concepts need to be strengthened, deepened, and clarified. In the following pages we seek to explore healing in a bit broader context than is customarily considered. For one thing, we consider it in the light of the holistic view of life and creation as seen in the Judeo-Christian tradition. We distinguish this from the dualism which prevailed in the Middle Ages and, to some extent, since. We also seek to explore it in the light of new perspectives gained by science, particularly of psychology and the awareness of the power of the subconscious. We seek to explore it especially in the context of the caring Christian fellowship such as must have been true in New Testament days.

Everywhere you look there is suffering and need. The offices of physicians, psychiatrists, and counselors are full of people seeking some cure for physical and emotional anguish. It seems a pity that, when the Church has in its custody such wonderful saving truth and such potential for loving, praying, believing support, it often has well-nigh forsaken that vital life-giving ministry of healing and left it in the hands of others.

We face the challenge of a future when great new insights will come. Let us bring together the power and love of God, the caring fellowship of his people, and the best insights we can gain, bringing healing to those who hurt.

Chapter 1

Creatures of Earth and Sky

WE HUMAN BEINGS are creatures of the earth as well as of the Spirit. We have earthly, physical bodies as well as that peculiar, God-given genius we call spirit. Genesis 2:7 says, "Then the Lord God formed man of dust from the ground, and breathed into his nostrils the breath of life; and man became a living being" (or soul). To deny either the earthly or the spiritual nature of a person is to deny the Holy Scriptures. We cannot close our eyes to what is manifestly, even painfully, apparent—that we are very earthy, physical beings. We have the insistent, demanding urges and drives of the animal, and we have the soul-stretching longings given us by our all-wise Creator. We are subject to the ravages of disease, to physical deterioration and decay, to accidents and the violent acts of nature, and to the hereditary factors which so largely "program" our bodies and, to some extent, our personalities. Whatever consideration we give to divine physical healing, then, must take account of our total nature. We cannot ignore the laws of nature and the fact of God in nature.

God of Law and Order

If God created the world and nature, then nature must reflect something of God himself. All through the Bible you see that sages, seers, and prophets reverenced and worshiped the Creator because of what they saw in his creation. The psalmist cried in reverence, "The heavens are telling the glory of God; and the firmament proclaims his handiwork. Day to day pours forth speech, and night to night declares knowledge. There is no speech, nor are there words; their voice is not heard; yet their voice goes out through all the earth, and their words to the end of the world" (Psa. 19:1-4). This is the silent language of nature which proclaims throughout the world that the Creator has ordained laws by which all nature operates. The Apostle Paul was so convinced of this that, when he wrote to the Romans, he insisted that even pagans, who had no knowledge of God such as the Jews had, would be nonetheless responsible: "For what can be known about God is plain to them, because God has shown it to them. Ever since the creation of the world his invisible nature, namely, his eternal power and deity, has been clearly perceived in the things that have been made. So they are without excuse . . ." (Rom. 1:19:20). Nature is God's creation.

If you look at the human body itself, you cannot help being impressed with its wonder and beauty, the delicate intricate balances, the mystery of procreation and birth, and the tremendous vitality of life. The laws of God are written within the physical processes, the tissues and cells, and we disregard those laws at our own peril.

All this tells us that God is not capricious or fickle. He is orderly. While many such physical laws are beyond our understanding, we can be sure that God's creation makes sense.

Cause and Effect

Things do not just happen. The principle of cause and effect is always in operation. For every effect there is a cause. Sometimes we speak of God himself as the "prime mover" or "original cause." Behind the changing scenes there is the Master of the show. We, of course, cannot see behind the scenes. We see only the surficial things; thus, our understanding is only a hint at what is really there. But we do know that this is not a capricious kind of universe. It operates by law, by cause and effect. We cannot assume that everything, no matter how trivial, is personally ordered by God according to some whim of the moment.

The principle of cause and effect is not limited to the purely physical, either. It surely must apply to what we may call spiritual laws. The fact is that we cannot separate the physical and spiritual, for life is one great whole.

Life Is a Rhythm

Life comes and goes in cycles: birth, life, reproduction, decline, and death. But death and decay help produce new life. Leaves spring out green and fresh; blossoms appear in all their variegated colors; fruit grows, ripens, then falls with its seed; leaves turn in color, drop to the ground, and become the fertilizer for new life and growth. Is one part of the cycle good and the other part evil? Seen in total perspective, it looks like all one beautiful plan.

In this process, nature is selective. Only the fittest survive. The weak are crowded out. Even whole species of life have become extinct. In the balance of nature one species of animal feeds on another, and that species on still another, and that one on certain vegetation. The ecological balance has prevailed for thousands of years and involves life in all its forms. Nature can be cruel and inexorable as its laws operate. And, let's face it, we are a part of this nature.

In the whole structure of nature and life, sensitivity plays a major part. The lowest forms of life know little or no pain. There are worms, for instance, which can be cut up into little pieces and each piece will grow into a whole worm. But at high levels of life the organism becomes more complex, sensitivity increases, and suffering is inevitably a part of life. Even in the human family there is a great range of sensitivity. The more sensitive we are, the more we are capable of both pleasure and pain. In human beings, fur-

9

thermore, pain can be mental and emotional as well as physical. Some of the greatest anguish is of that kind. Pain is even necessary. It is our signal that something is wrong. Were it not for pain we would not know when to seek help. Thus, aging, pain, sickness, and death are a part of the cycle of life as the laws of nature operate impartially. We human beings have common ground with all other forms of life.

Causes of Suffering

There are many reasons why people suffer pain. There are hereditary factors which leave some people with weak or deformed bodies. There are economic and social factors which deny many thousands the proper nourishment and shelter. There are diseases which infect the body bringing temporary or permanent illness. There are the abuses by which we bring upon ourselves unnecessary illness: overwork; overeating; use of poisonous substances like nicotine, alcohol, drugs, and so on. There are the accidents which befall us, sometimes through our own or someone else's carelessness. There are the violent acts of nature like volcanoes, earthquakes, tornadoes, or floods. Then there are the tensions, stresses, anxieties, and worries which may bring on heart attacks or high blood pressure. (To worry yourself to death may not be as spectacular as shooting yourself through the head—but it's just as permanent, and a lot more painful!)

There are causes of suffering which we can correct. There are some over which we have no control. To recognize the laws of nature and to respect those laws could relieve us of much of the suffering in the world. We might well give more attention to intelligent cooperation with nature's laws before questioning an all-wise God and his goodness. He gave us eyes and ears and minds to use in learning all we can about those laws. An unduly mystical interpretation of what befalls us can be a hindrance to the common sense realism so necessary to live in harmony with the laws of God in nature.

Vitality of Life

On the positive side of all this is the tremendous vitality and adaptability of life. In recent years we have been informed by some very fine television presentations on wildlife and the balance of nature. One can hardly help being impressed with the countless forms of life across the whole gamut, from the tiniest insects to the most pondorous creatures of the land and sea. And they show only a very small fraction of the forms life takes. You can't set your foot down without treading on life—even though it is too small to see. The earth is literally bursting with life of all kinds.

Then there is the persistence of life. Some creatures survive under the most harsh and hostile conditions, guided by some marvelous instinct that enables them to adapt to changing conditions, to avoid being consumed by predators, to build their homes and care for their young. To observe the powerful, instinctual mating urges and the sometimes elaborate performances of the mating process is to see how powerful is the procreative nature and how very necessary to the survival of the species. The care and training of the young is marvelous to behold. True, there is death lurking behind the bush but the young are taught the dangers. True, many die in the predator's jaws but nature provides an abundance of offspring and the species generally lives on. What if there were no death? Soon the overpopulation would bring the death of all.

Healing Is Part of Nature

The physical body, including the human body, has tremendous recuperative powers. The animal that is wounded is driven by instinct to seek shelter, to eat only what is needed, and to rest, giving the body its optimum chance to be restored. Who teaches the animal all this? No one. It is a built-in capacity.

Archaeological finds have shown that recovery has been made even when severe bodily damage has been inflicted. This is true of both animal bodies and human bodies. Healing is not foreign to nature. This amazing resilience in life is true all across the spectrum.

Plants heal as well as animals. Lightning may strike a tree and split it. Unless it is damaged too badly, the tree recuperates and the wound heals over. A branch is cut off and the wound heals over. You cut your finger and very shortly healing begins. A wound becomes infected and the blood forms pus as a protective device.

Physicians know full well that they themselves have no healing power, and the drugs they administer are only to counteract the poison or correct the obstruction. Nature itself does the healing.

The earth itself has healing qualities. The sun is a great healer. These, along with the herbs and plants having medicinal qualities, are a part of nature itself. Healing is taking place all the time in plants, in animals, in marine life, in the fowl of the air, and in the human body. We should not think it strange, then, that healing is a part of God's plan for us. All healing must surely be from God, the Author of nature. This is not to say that all such healing is what we would call "divine healing," but that healing is not foreign to God's creation. It is part of the whole cycle of life that he has created.

Physical and Spiritual

In human beings we must consider more than the physical body alone, for we are more than animals. The highly developed nervous system with its marvelous instrument, the brain, makes us a different kind of being. The spiritual nature given by God puts us in a whole new dimension. We have the powers of choice, of imagination, of memory, of sustained attention, of faith or unbelief. It is well known that our mental and emotional climate powerfully affects our bodies. Physicians say that a high percentage of those

12

who are ill have really a mentally or emotionally induced illness. Estimates are that fifty percent (and up to ninety percent) of the hospital patients are suffering from psychosomatic (mind-body) disorders. The mind has a very great influence on the body, and vice versa.

It is apparent, then, that to consider healing we have to think in the broader context of the laws of nature and of the complex nature of persons. The Bible does just that. It is fitting that we approach this consideration with reverence and with appreciation for all that our Creator has provided—not in an overly-simplistic or rigid way, and certainly not in a demanding or condemning way. Life is one beautiful whole and it is given by God. His revealed will in his Holy Word will be our guide.

For Discussion

1. In what sense are we to understand that we, as human beings, are creatures of earth and of the Spirit? Is the human being an animal? What more?

2. If God is a personal God touched by our needs, does that mean he overrules the natural laws? How do you harmonize your conception of God and of physical laws?

3. If we, as human beings, are part of the natural order, can we expect to 'be exempt from the sometimes cruel forces of nature?

4. How do you see divine healing fitting into the creation of law, of cause and effect, and such? Does this seeming incongruity affect your faith?

Personal Notes

.

Chapter 2

Healing and Wholeness in the Bible

THE INFINITE God who created nature and life surely is able to heal and renew life. It is not strange, therefore, that we find references to physical healing in the divine record. While healing comes into clearer and more vivid focus in the New Testament, especially in the ministry of Jesus, it is seen in the Old Testament as well. It is part of God's unfolding plan for his people. Before tracing that, however, it will be helpful for us to observe some basic concepts in which healing is to be understood.

God Is Present

The Creator did not wind up creation like a clock and then sit down in some splendid distance to wait until it ran down. He is present in his creation. He sustains his work. He is "upholding the universe by his word of power" (Heb. 1:3). Theologians use the word *omnipresent* to say that God is present in all places at all times. "Whither shall I go from thy Spirit?" cried the psalmist, "Or whither shall I flee from thy presence? If I ascend to heaven, thou art there! If I make my bed in Sheol, thou art there! If I take the wings of the morning and dwell in the uttermost parts of the sea, even there thy hand shall lead me, and thy right hand shall hold me" (Psa. 139:7-10).

15

God is! He is real, and he is present. When Moses was sent to Pharaoh to secure the deliverance of the Israelite people, he was overwhelmed with the size of the assignment. "If I come to the people of Israel," he lamented, "and say to them, 'The God of your fathers has sent me to you' and they ask me, 'What is his name?' what shall I say to them?" God said to Moses, "I AM WHO I AM." And he said, "Say this to the people of Israel, 'I AM has sent me to you' " (Exod. 3:13-14).

If God is present, then, he must be present in his fullness, for he is *one* God, present *as he is*. He never loses the identity of being. He is not fragmented. And he is not capricious. He is unchanging, eternal. He is the same in every age. He is always available. God *is*!

He Is Present in All of Life

In the Bible and in Hebrew thinking you do not see a false separation of the physical and the spiritual. It is all one world, one creation. The false dualism came from other cultures. In New Testament times it was the main heresy the Church had to contend with. More about that later. The point here is that all God's creation is united in one great reality. This means that human and physical affairs are God's concern just as spiritual things are. Every part of life is to be under his control.

It is logical, therefore, that God's covenant with Israel included provision for the body. It dealt with physical habits, cleanliness, diet, and measures to assure the survival of Jewish culture. Through the illustrious leader, Moses, God gave them this promise: "If you will diligently hearken to the voice of the Lord your God, and do that which is right in his eyes, and give heed to his commandments and keep all his statutes, I will put none of the diseases upon you which I put upon the Egyptians; for I am the Lord, your healer" (Exod. 15:26). In a number of instances this was affirmed to them. (See Exod. 23:20-25; Deut. 7:15; 28:58, 61.)

It is quite clear that God was concerned with all of life; the spiritual, the physical, the social, and the national. In considering this, we must remember that he was preparing the way for his Son to make known his will more fully. When you turn to the New Testament and the ministry of Jesus, you see in full glory the concern God has for all of life, for Jesus touched people at the place of their need, no matter what it might have been.

Promise of Healing in Prophecy

In keeping with God's purpose, the concern for all of life comes through in the prophecies. The prophets were not bashful about addressing very human, physical problems. They rebuked those who made religion a separate thing— something that took place in the Temple by the ceremonies and rituals of the priestly class. They demanded justice be- fore the law, fair weights and measures, fair and charitable treatment of the poor, and so on. Bodies counted as well as souls.

Nowhere does this total concern come through more clearly than in Isaiah's prophecy: "The Spirit of the Lord God is upon me, because the Lord has anointed me to bring good tidings to the afflicted; he has sent me to bind up the brokenhearted, to proclaim liberty to the captives, and the opening of the prison to those who are bound; to proclaim the year of the Lord's favor, and the day of vengeance of our God; to comfort all who mourn . . ." (61:1-2). That covers life as a whole. It doesn't sound like something "spiritual" removed from everyday life.

And this is precisely the passage Jesus read in the synagogue in Nazareth as he launched into his earthly ministry. Luke records it (4:18-19) and adds Jesus' com- ment as "the eyes of all in the synagogue were fixed on him . . ." He said, "Today this scripture has been fulfilled in your hearing" (vv. 20-21). He plainly accepted the thrust of the prophets' concern as his own commitment.

Many passages in the prophecies contain allusions and

17

direct references to God's care for physical and social life. Liberation was to be for the whole person. The thinking was holistic, not dualistic, and it was theistic, not humanistic. Matthew, who saw so much direct relationship between the prophecies and the ministry of Jesus, cites the instance where he had healed Peter's mother-in-law. He says, "many [came] who were possessed with demons; and he cast out the spirits with a word, and healed all who were sick." Then he adds: "This was to fulfill what was spoken by the prophet Isaiah, 'He took our infirmities and bore our diseases' " (Matt. 8:16-17). Thus, in both Old and New Testaments the same steady purpose is continued—to minister to the whole person.

Instances of Healing

Since the next chapter will be discussing healing in the ministry of Jesus, our purpose here is only to show that there were indeed instances of healing in the Old Testament times and that the idea was always a part of God's plan. We turn simply to a few examples of such healing.

The first is that of Naaman, commander of the army of the king of Syria—not a Jew but one who reverenced the Lord. Second Kings 5 gives us the account. Naaman was a victim of the most dreaded disease—leprosy. A little girl who had been taken as a captive from Israel was a personal servant of Naaman's wife. She told him of the prophet Elisha and advised him to seek healing. The story is a familiar one and need not be repeated here, but the humbling experience of a "great" man does deserve reflection. The strange command to dip seven times in the muddy Jordan River called for simple obedience, and that is a lesson in itself. In any case, Naaman was healed.

One more instance will do. Second Kings 20 gives us this account: Hezekiah was at the point of death. Isaiah, the prophet, gave him the Lord's word, "Set your house in order; for you shall die, you shall not recover" (v. 1). But Hezekiah turned his face to the wall and prayed, weeping inconsolably. Then the prophet received another word from the Lord. "Turn back, and say to Hezekiah . . . I have heard your prayer, I have seen your tears; behold, I will heal you . . . I will add fifteen years to your life" (vv. 5:5).

God's power was more in the form of certain visitations for healing in the Old Testament. In the New Testament it becomes a normal part of divine ministry. While somewhat incipient in the earlier days, God's plan was nonetheless apparent and real. Healing was definitely a part of his covenant with Israel. "I am the Lord, your healer" (Exod. 15:26b).

Healing, Physical and Spiritual

We love to hear the beautiful and assuring affirmation in Psalm 103:1-4: "Bless the Lord, O my soul . . . and forget not all his benefits, who forgives all your iniquity, who heals all your diseases." Remember that was chanted for hundreds of years before the time of Jesus. The healing of body and soul are linked together. This always had been true but here we see it in sharp focus. In the New Testament, of course, it was even more apparent. The preaching of the gospel and healing of the sick were part of the same ministry, in Jesus himself and in the charge he gave to his followers. It shows up in Jesus' healing of the paralytic in Capernaum, as recorded in Mark 2:1-12: "My son, your sins are forgiven . . . Rise, take up your pallet and go home" (v. 5). They are like two sides of a coin. In the instruction of James 5:13-16 we are told that "the prayer of faith will save the sick . . . and if he has committed sins, he will be forgiven. Therefore confess your sins to one another, and pray for one another, that you may be healed." We will return to this important principle later, for God's plan includes both physical and spiritual healing.

Sickness and Sin

On the negative side, there has been the association of

sickness with sin. "Who sinned," asked the disciples of Jesus, "this man or his parents, that he was born blind?" (John 9:1-2). Of course, Jesus corrected their wrong notion but their thinking was typical. There was a common belief that sickness was sent by God as a punishment for sin.

This was the great argument in the Book of Job. The "friends" and "comforters" persisted with the idea that Job's afflictions were the consequence of some sin he had committed. Job stoutly defended himself and argued the question because he knew better. Even today there are such "friends" who add condemnation to the affliction and aggravate the burden of the sick.

There is indeed a relationship between sin and sickness, but not necessarily personal sin. Rather, it is sin in the generic sense—the sinful condition. Human beings are part of the sinful society with its often degenerate practices. The sins of the fathers often are visited upon the children "to the third and fourth generation," as the First Commandment says. But it is wrong to condemn a sick person by assuming that there is some personal sin in his or her life. There is a difference between the state or condition of sin and the personal sin which brings guilt upon the soul.

Nonetheless we suffer in many ways as the result of sin. There is a solidarity in the human race. No one is an independent entity separate from the rest. We are all in this together, like it or not. And the fact that you are a Christian does not make you immune.

A Concept of Healing

To develop an adequate doctrine of healing would require much more treatment than we can give it here. Some basic conceptions may help, however.

What is sickness? Is it God's will or not? The attitude of the Bible, especially the New Testament, is that sickness is evil. Its origin lies in the disobedience to divine laws, the lack of harmony with the laws of God and of his creation. Exodus 15:26 gives us this basic concept early. Jesus treated sickness as an evil to overcome. In healing a sick person Jesus made that person a participant in God's will. Liberation from sickness and sin was one operation.

The Resurrection signals Christ's victory over the "last enemy which is death." Thus, the whole life and ministry, death and Resurrection of our Lord is the act of the Almighty God in restoring a mortal, sinful person to wholeness and abundant life. This includes all of life—body, mind, and soul. It allows no compartmentalizing of life. The lordship of Christ is over all.

Physical healing has been an integral part of God's plan all across the generations. It was a part of his covenant with Israel. It was promised by the prophets. It was, in Hebrew history, at least an occasional reality in experience. In Jesus Christ it came into full expression. He charged his apostles to continue in the same work, preaching salvation and healing to all the world.

For Discussion

1. What is meant by the "holistic" view of life, in contrast to the "dualistic" view? Check the dictionary for these meanings and see how you view life. What difference does it make in our beliefs about the body and about healing?

2. In what sense are sickness and sin related? If a person is sick, is that an indication of sin in his or her life? What of the person who has been prayed for but has not been healed?

3. How do you understand the relationship between healing and forgiveness? If a person is healed, is that person always forgiven, also?

4. State briefly your conception of healing. Do the members of your group basically agree on this?

Personal Notes

Chapter 3

Healing in the Ministry of Jesus

IF ONE were to point out any one thing in which Jesus majored, it probably would be healing. To read the Gospels is to see how "he went about doing good," opening blind eyes, unstopping deaf ears, raising up the dying and even the dead. The list is almost endless. If John's last comment is to be taken seriously there must be a great deal of which we have no record, for he said, "There are also many other things which Jesus did; were every one of them to be written, I suppose that the world itself could not contain the books that would be written" (John 21:25). Now, assuming that much of what was not written was physical healing, that's a lot of healing!

The healing miracles largely catapulted Jesus into prominence. After the searching experience of fasting and prayer in the wilderness for forty days and nights, and the onslaughts of Satan in the three great tests, Jesus apparently had done quite a few healings. At least Luke records how "Jesus returned in the power of the Spirit into Galilee, and a report concerning him went out through all the surrounding country" (Luke 4:14). Immediately his name was on everyone's lips. The many thousands of people who were sick and desperate turned eagerly to him. Pathetic people—malnourished, poor, disease-ridden—stretched out their arms, pleading for his help. It was not a pretty sight, we can be sure of that.

He Was Moved with Compassion

Jesus was magnetic. Wherever he went, all eyes were fixed on him. Hostile eyes. Pleading eyes. Skeptical eyes. He saw it all, and he was undismayed, for he saw people "like sheep having no shepherd" (Matt. 9:36). They were "lost" in different ways. They had many different kinds of problems. Jesus looked upon every one of them with that great love in his heart which can come only from God who is love. He looked upon people with deep compassion. He carried a sob in his heart.

And they felt that. Here was one person in all the world who really cared about them. No doubt their whole outlook was changed and their faith inspired just to be in his presence. What a change it must have been for those who had seen so much of condemning legalism and so many frowning priests and rulers! Here was sheer love. Jesus was like a shaft of pure, golden sunlight through the clouds on a murky and dark day. Love must have shone from his eyes. His hands must have had the tender strength that brought great comfort and courage to their hearts.

Some have thought that Jesus performed healings and other miracles mainly to gain publicity and thus get his message across. But that is quite unthinkable. For one thing it would have to be a little less than authentic and sincere. But even more it was unnecessary because love was the *message*. Wholeness was the *objective*.

No, while his healings did bring recognition and his ministry was authenticated by them to many people, we have to conclude that Jesus healed because he loved—far more than we can know. Divine love and spiritual energy flowed from him and it was expressed largely through his healing ministry. And love is to human life what light is to a plant. It is creative. Love, in the way Jesus expressed it, was divine. It did not merely respond to value and worth as does our human love. It *created* value. It *imparted* worth. Such love allowed no limits to be set upon it by a person's worthiness or unworthiness. It was *unconditional*. It was unmerited favor. It is impossible for us to imagine what that meant to people who had never known real love and care. It was a revelation.

Perhaps the most fundamental requirement—really the highest privilege—in receiving healing is simply *accepting* God's love, *believing* that he loves us. Real faith for healing is predicated on the acceptance of that love and upon acceptance of the idea that God loves the whole person, body as well as mind, and soul.

Jesus Saw Life Whole

Earlier we insisted that, in the Hebrew teaching and tradition, life was holistic—that is, it was all one. There was no artificial separation between the physical body and the spiritual nature, nor between the physical world and the spiritual. Jesus' ministry was within this tradition and belief. He saw life whole. His ministry was to bring people to wholeness.

Already we have cited the synagogue experience in Nazareth, as recorded in Luke 4, where Jesus stood up to read from Isaiah 61. "The Spirit of the Lord God is upon me, because he has anointed me. . . ." He claimed this as his own commission saying, "Today this scripture has been fulfilled in your hearing." The commission included preaching "good news to the poor," proclaiming "release to the captives," and "recovering of sight to the blind," "setting at liberty those who were oppressed," and "proclaiming the acceptable year of the Lord." (The last reference here was to the year of Jubilee when captives were released and crimes forgiven.)

This commission manifestly relates to life as a whole. It includes physical needs, social problems, and spiritual rebirth. It is significant that Jesus announced this as the thrust of his ministry. The objective was wholeness of life and the glory of God.

Jesus' view of sickness was that the whole person was ill, not just the body. The problem was alienation from God and persons. Wholeness was being in right relationship with

God and others. Therefore physical healing and forgiveness go together. "Thy sins be forgiven thee," he said—and almost in the same breath, "Take up your bed and go home." No, the combination is not always seen just that way, but there surely was this total impact in his ministry. It is important that this be also the focus of our ministry in his name.

Jesus came to do not his own will, but the will of his Father. Always he lived and taught and acted *as the Son.* He declared: "My food is to do the will of him who sent me, and to accomplish his work" (John 4:34). "Believe me that I am in the Father and the Father in me; or else believe me for the sake of the works themselves" (John 14:11). "We must work the works of him who sent me, while it is day; night comes, when no one can work. As long as I am in the world, I am the light of the world" (John 9:4-5). Referring to John the Baptist, Jesus said, "The testimony which I have is greater than that of John; for the works which the Father has granted me to accomplish, these very works which I am doing, bear me witness that the Father has sent me" (John 5:36).

Therefore, if we accept what Jesus himself said, we cannot question the fact that he regarded all his acts of healing as willed by the Father. They were indeed a sign of his compassion, for Jesus always took upon himself the burdens, the suffering, and the heartache of those who came to him. The importance which he gave to healing constitutes a convincing, visible sign of the redemptive love of God the Father. It was full redemption—the salvation of the whole human being—physical healing being an important element of it.

According to the account in Genesis, the first man's sin separated him from God; it resulted in spiritual death. This spiritual break left in its wake guilt, condemnation, sickness, suffering, alienation, and death. It is the sign of our sinful state—our separation from the Source of life. Redemption, then, had to include restoration to spiritual and physical wholeness. That is in keeping with our nature as

God created us. "Then the Lord God formed man of the dust from the ground, and breathed into his nostrils the breath of life; and man became a living being" (Gen. 2:7).

Sickness Is Evil

The Gospels give ample evidence that, in Jesus' view, sickness is the work of Satan. The fact that he cured many people's illnesses by casting out demons surely proves that he regarded them as being of satanic origin. Today, most diseases have been classified and defined, studied and treated scientifically. Even the biblical cases of demon possession often are explained today as mental and emotional disorders. But Jesus branded it otherwise. "Ought not this woman, a daughter of Abraham whom Satan bound for eighteen years," he asked, "be loosed from this bond [even] on the sabbath day?" (Luke 13:16). And that was not a case of demon possession, either—it was a bent back. But it was not a part of God's plan for her.

When Jesus healed a blind and dumb demoniac, some Pharisees accused him of casting out demons by the power of Beelzebub, the prince of demons. His reply was that such an idea was self-contradictory. It would be Satan working against Satan. (See Matt. 12:22-26.) Here also sickness is regarded as being of satanic origin. There was a vital relationship between sin and sickness and between forgiveness and healing. Jesus affirmed healing as a part of the divine plan. It was not incidental but integral in his ministry.

Sick People Are Not to Be Condemned

The basic association of sickness with the sinful condition, which was valid enough, led to the erroneous conclusion that if a person was sick it was because of that person's sin. Job argued strenuously on this point, as you will remember.

27

"Who sinned," asked the disciples, "this man or his parents, that he was born blind?" The inference is clear: If one is blind it must be because of one's sin. But no sickness is related to the whole sinful condition and the fall from fellowship with God; yet no person is to be condemned or accused of personal sin because of sickness. Great harm has been done by such condemnation, and good people have been burdened even further because of the insensitivity and misinformation of some who seem to feel called upon to pronounce judgment.

If a person acts contrary to the laws of God—whether through ignorance, folly, or sin—that person does have to bear certain consequences in the suffering of body, mind, and emotions. There often is a quite direct cause-effect relationship. (Lung cancer is allegedly linked to tobacco smoke, for instance.) But not all sickness can be said to result from this cause-effect relationship. As a part of the great human family we may suffer liabilities that we do not individually deserve just as we enjoy certain blessings and assets which we did not personally earn. "No man is an island," said John Donne. Each of us is linked to the great mainland of humanity. It is in this broader sense that sickness is related to sin—or rather, to the sinful condition.

So when we see Christ healing as well as forgiving, we have evidence that the intention of God is health and wholeness. Two heresies rob us of living faith. One is that the sick person is under condemnation because of personal sin. Another is that sickness is "normal" or that God sends sickness upon us for our spiritual growth or discipline. Nowhere does Jesus either condemn the sick or urge people to live with their sickness. He healed them! Healing was a unique expression of God's love.

His Methods of Healing

Jesus used no one method or approach in healing the sick. He had no single formula. His divine sensitivity enabled him to know, in each case, what was needed and to touch the trigger that would inspire faith. Sometimes he seemed to use what a psychologist today would call *suggestion*. Four examples would be: the cleansing of the leper (Mark 1:40-45), the ten lepers (Luke 17:11-19), the woman with the hemorrhage (Mark 5:25-34), and the man at the pool of Bethesda (John 5:1-18). He used a different approach with the demoniac (Mark 5:1-20) and the man "possessed" at Capernaum (Mark 1:23-28). Such instances as Jairus' daughter (Matt. 9:18-26), the centurion's son, and the nobleman's slave (which could be different accounts of the same incident—see Matt. 8:5-13, Luke 7:1-10, John 4:46-54), seem to involve the faith of other persons. These instances should be sufficient to indicate that our Lord made a different and creative approach in each case. A thorough investigation of this by a responsible scholar would inform us all.

Jesus' ministry, then, was one directed toward the wholeness of each person. That included physical healing, which seemed to be a unique and special expression of his great compassion and redemptive power.

For Discussion

1. Why do you think Jesus did so much healing? What was his purpose in it?

2. What method(s) did Jesus use in healing, and why? How can we understand his various approaches to people? Can we use his methods?

3. Do you feel uneasy about this business of healing today? Can we realistically hope for results? Where and how do we most often miss it?

4. How much did Jesus' special divine insight have to do with his healings? Can we develop any such discernment? or is the "gift of discernment" operable in this connection?

Personal Notes

Chapter 4

Healing in the Early Church

JESUS left no question or uncertainty about his intention that such healing work as he had done should go on after his own earthly ministry was over. His promise was breathtaking: "Truly, truly, I say to you, he who believes in me will also do the works that I do; and greater works than these will he do, because I go to the Father. Whatever you ask in my name, I will do it, that the Father may be glorified in the Son" (John 14:12-13). According to Matthew's account, he had sent out the Twelve with the clear instruction to "heal the sick, raise the dead, cleanse lepers, cast out demons" (Matt. 10:8).

He himself had set the example before them and demonstrated the power of God. How very aware they must have been of his own ministry as, in the early church, they sought to carry on the work he did! When they were gathered together in the Upper Room prior to the Pentecost experience, they were faced with the need to choose another person to take the place of Judas who had defected. They recognized some basic requirements that such a person would have to meet. He would have to be "one of the men who have accompanied us during all the time that the Lord Jesus went in and out among us, beginning from the baptism of John until the day when he was taken up from us—one of these men must become with us a witness to the

31

resurrection'' (Acts 1:21-22). In short, the twelve apostles were men who had lived with Jesus and worked with him intimately, and who were witnesses to his Resurrection. They had to be fully aware of Jesus' teaching, healing, and saving power. Jesus was still central. He had promised to always be with them. They lived in the freshness and excitement of the Resurrection, along with the personal impact of his spirit upon their lives. From the very first, healing was an integral part of the Church's ministry.

Healing through the Apostles

Right after the Day of Pentecost, "Peter and John were going up to the temple at the hour of prayer, the ninth hour. And a man lame from birth was being carried, whom they laid daily at that gate of the temple which is called Beautiful to ask alms of those who entered the temple . . . And Peter directed his gaze at him, with John, and said, 'Look at us' . . . Peter said, 'I have no silver and gold, but I give you what I have; in the name of Jesus Christ of Nazareth, walk.' And he took him by the right hand and raised him up; and immediately his feet and ankles were made strong. And leaping up he stood and walked and entered the temple with them, walking and leaping and praising God" (Acts 3:1-8). The immediate result was "wonder and amazement"—and persecution!

The Acts of the Apostles is a record replete with accounts of healing, miraculous deliverance, powerful influence, rebuking of evil, and contagious evangelistic spirit. "Now many signs and wonders were done among the people," says the account, "by the hands of the apostles." The quality of fellowship and spiritual power was so great among them that "none of the rest dared join them, but the people held them in high honor" (Acts 5:12). It was a time of tremendous spiritual vitality arising out of simple faith. (One should add that certainly it was not Peter's *shadow* that healed anybody, but the power of God through their childlike faith.)

Healing Not Limited to The Apostles

While the twelve apostles seemed to have a special faith for healing, others also prayed for the sick with success. For instance, Paul was powerfully used in such ministry. At Lystra a man who had been badly crippled from the very time of his birth was healed when Paul commanded, "Stand upright on your feet." The record says that "he sprang up and walked" (Acts 14:10). The crowd was so electrified that some claimed Paul and his companion Barnabas were gods. But Paul and Barnabas stoutly protested that they were only the servants of the living God who had created all things.

Always the healing was in the name of Jesus. The early Christians never attempted miracles in their own power. They knew better than that. They went as the representatives of Jesus, the Christ. They gave to him all the glory. A careful reading of the Acts of the Apostles will convince us that the power of God by the name of Jesus was very real and demonstrable in the first-century church.

There was a significant use of united prayer and faith. Jesus had promised that "if two of you [even two!] agree on earth about anything they ask, it will be done for them by my Father in heaven. For where two or three are gathered in my name, there am I in the midst of them" (Matt. 18:19-20). There seemed to be a special focus of power in *agreement*, in the uniting of minds, in the mutual support of faith. Throughout the New Testament this power of agreement and focused concern is seen. It must be one of our major emphases in the consideration of healing and other miracles.

When Peter and John faced the scowling Sanhedrin, boldly declaring that the lame man had been healed by the power of Jesus, they did so with a group of praying people behind them. When Peter, who had been thrown into prison, was delivered by God's power, it was because a group of believers had gathered and prayed as one. That was the secret of much of the power in the early church—a secret now sometimes overlooked.

Gifts of the Spirit

It was Paul, apostle to the Gentile world, who wrote most about the gifts of the Spirit. In his letter to the Christian believers in Corinth, he gave a rather full list of these spiritual gifts (though one notices that his three lists in Romans 12, 1 Corinthians 12, and Ephesians 4 are not identical, leading to the impression that these lists are suggestive rather than exhaustive). Among the gifts he listed were those of healing and the working of miracles (1 Cor. 12:9-10).

According to Paul, a gift of the Spirit is an equipment for service. The gift of healing, then, was the divinely given capacity for compassion and faith as a means of healing. Likewise the gift of working miracles. Healing was a normal part of the ministry of the Church in that time, just as much as prophecy or knowledge or wisdom. Healing was not the speciality of peripheral cults or glamour personalities or other tangential movements. It was very much a normal function of the fellowship. One can imagine their meetings as they gathered—often secretly—in homes or wherever they could. Knit together in deep fellowship of the Spirit, desperately needing the support of praying and loving friends, they faced the hostility and persecution; they brought their cares and burdens, their bodily illness and suffering into the redemptive atmosphere of love. One can imagine some of the beloved leaders gathering around the suffering one with the whole group united in believing love. They apparently had the custom of laying their hands on the sick after anointing with oil. We have no way to know very much about their actual customs. But we may safely surmise that they were informal and personal in their relationships, probably with a great deal of sharing of their experiences and lives.

Call for the Elders

It was James—the down-to-earth, practical man—who

gave the most specific instruction we have on record with regard to praying for the sick. "Is any among you sick? Let him call for the elders of the church, and let them pray over him, anointing him with oil in the name of the Lord; and the prayer of faith will save the sick man, and the Lord will raise him up; and if he has committed sins, he will be forgiven. Therefore confess your sins to one another, and pray for one another, that you may be healed" (James 5:14-16a).

This was not intended as a ritual to be observed or a ceremony to be carried out. It is the common-sense instruction for an orderly way to bring the greatest dimension of meaning and faith. It was to take place in the fellowship of loving, believing friends. The call or request for prayer was made by the sick one. It was at his or her own initiation, no doubt after some personal preparation, for the apostle had just said, "Is any one among you suffering? Let him pray . . ." (v. 13). The person was to pray for himself or herself first, then call for the elders (natural leaders) of the Christian fellowship. The prayer for healing was more than a lonely, individual prayer. The whole body of believers shared in the burden.

In the instruction also is the provision for open confession of needs, problems, and heartaches—even of faults and sins. That is sound advice. Healing takes place in an atmosphere of honesty and openness. Confession is often the prerequisite to healing. And when the healing comes, forgiveness comes also. This intimate association between physical and spiritual healing is not strange in the Bible. As pointed out before, physical and spiritual healing go together. The preaching of redemption in Christ is accompanied by healing. It is God "who forgiveth all thine iniquities, who healeth all thy diseases."

Resurrection Power

According to the New Testament, the whole healing ministry related to the reality of the Resurrection of the

Lord who was regnantly present among his subjects in his "body," the Church. He acted in and through the Church in the same manner and with the same power as he did during his physical presence and ministry among them. So it was that, in accordance with the clear commands of its Lord, the Church carried forward the ministry of Christ himself. "He that believeth on me," Jesus had said, "the works that I do shall he do also." The early church conceived its mission in those terms.

So for the first century church the healing of the sick was an integral part of the message and mission. It was one of the most powerful signs of his authenticating presence and power.

In the Roman letter, Paul explains the direct relationship between the Resurrection and the new life given to the believer. "If the Spirit of him who raised Jesus from the dead dwells in you, he who raised Christ Jesus from the dead will give life to your mortal bodies also through his Spirit which dwells in you" (8:11). While this text does not refer primarily to physical healing, the principle is there and it manifestly bears meaning for healing.

Elements of Healing

Nowhere does the New Testament give us, in order, the essential elements of healing. But we can see some basic elements in it nonetheless. The first surely would be *compassion*. The Lord Jesus was "moved with compassion" again and again. He cared. He gravitated to the needy, the sick, the lonely, and the lost. The early Christians deeply cared for one another.

Peter and John, at the gate of the Temple, fixed their eyes on the lame man and said, "Look at us." *Contact!* There was something deeply personal and compassionate in their dealings.

Healings were totally dependent upon *the power of the resurrected Christ*. "Silver and gold have I none," said Peter to the lame man, "but such as I have give I thee. In the name of Jesus Christ of Nazareth. . . ." That was the crux of their message and the secret of their success. Everything they said and did was in His name.

There was authority in that name. They said, "In the name of Jesus Christ of Nazareth, walk." Peter knew himself to be a representative of Jesus' name. It was by Jesus' authority that he was given authority. His was a derived authority. The true authority was Jesus Christ.

The phenomenal events of the New Testament can be understood only by knowing how absolutely central Jesus was in the fellowship of believers. Wherever two or three were gathered together in his name, there he was also. The Healer himself was among them.

For Discussion

1. What did the early church have that we do not have? anything?

2. Was divine healing to be limited to the apostolic days? When Jesus said, "Greater works than these shall ye do," did he mean us? Did he have reference to quality of works? or to quantity?

3. Do only certain persons have access to divine healing powers? Only those with the "gift" of healing? What about the rest of us?

4. What special value is there in agreement among two or more persons when we pray for the sick?

Personal Notes

Chapter 5

Healing Across the Generations

FOR ABOUT three hundred years divine healing was a part of the ministry of the early Christian church. Gradually the emphasis upon it waned, but it did not completely disappear. A general observation would be that, in its times of greater spiritual power, the Church has always experienced instances of healing. Of course—then as now—there were deeply devoted people who experienced the power of God while, at the same time, others seemed content with only a nominal form of Christianity. Then as now, some congregations would be more spiritually vital than others. Presumably much depended upon the leaders they had.

The Patristic Period

Dr. Bernard Martin has given us a brief look at some of the Church fathers and their convictions about healing. It will be helpful to look at just a few brief statements.[1]

Hermas, writing about 140 A.D. stressed healing. "Not only is it a great joy to free men from the sufferings afflicting them," he said, "but to know that they are suffering and not to attempt to free them is a great sin."

Tatian, who wrote at about the same time, insisted that it was not right to attribute the healing of the sick to material things. He felt that faith in the medicinal value of roots and herbs diverted the mind from gratitude to God. "For what reason," he asked, "do you not approach the more powerful Lord but rather seek to heal yourself like the dog with grass or the stag with a viper? Yield to the power of the Logos." (Presumably, he used *Logos* to mean Christ, the "Word made flesh," in keeping with John's term in the fourth Gospel.)

Irenaeus, about 180 A.D., stressed the healings that only Christians were capable of accomplishing by faith. He mentioned restoring of sight to the blind and hearing to the deaf, casting out devils, healing the paralytic, and even raising the dead. For "as the Lord raised them, and the apostles did by means of prayer," so the Church should retain such power. "Those who are in truth His disciples, receiving grace from Him, do in His name perform miracles . . . according to the gift which each one has received from Him." He went on to stress that, by the laying on of hands, many were healed and blessed. The gift of healing was still being exercised nearly two hundred years after Jesus' earthly ministry.

Origen, who lived until 254 A.D., said, "There are still preserved among Christians traces of that Holy Spirit which appeared in the form of a dove" (referring, no doubt, to the time of Jesus' baptism). He said that there were evidences of healing and of prophecy still in the church of that day. "We assert," he said, "that the whole habitable world contains evidence of the work of Jesus."

Augustine, as late as the fifth century A.D., mentions miracles which he himself witnessed. Thus there were many instances of healing long after the days of the twelve apostles. However, there was a general decline in the emphasis upon healing and the evidence of divine power; and at the same time there was a trend toward more ecclesiastical structure and controls. The Church became less dependent upon the inspiration of the Holy Spirit and more dependent upon organization—less spiritual and more humanistic. The trend away from pure, simple faith and awareness of Christ's own power and toward the increasing dependence on human resources and wisdom continued through the long centuries that followed, with only some isolated instances of real spiritual power. Much later new light and vitality was to dawn once more.

A Wrong View of Life

Earlier we observed that, in the Hebrew teaching and tradition, all of life was held to be sacred. God the Creator had made the first man from the dust of the earth and breathed into his nostrils the breath of life. Human beings were meant to live in fellowship with God and under his lordship. The home and family life was to be sacred. One's vocation was a sacred duty before God. Common everyday affairs and work, fairness in trade and commerce—all were a part of life under God. The prophets cried out against any form of worship that overlooked fairness and justice. The lordship of God was over all these things.

Jesus lived and taught in that tradition. He dignified common labor by his own involvement in it. He cared about people's bodies as well as their souls. His ministry was to make people whole. To him, sickness was evil. So he healed the sick. He regarded the body as the temple of God. "Know ye not that the kingdom of God is within you?" he asked.

But there prevailed in the pagan teaching of that time the idea that all material things were evil, that the whole world was evil, that the human body was evil. Therefore, the body was to them not the temple of the spirit but its *prison*. Dr. William Barclay, the noted New Testament scholar, has pointed our repeatedly in his writings that this belief (Gnosticism) was the major heresy confronting the Church in that day and was, to some extent, infiltrating the Church. Such people believed that a holy God would never have sent his Son to such an evil world. They denied the incarnation and the divinity of Jesus. It was to this heresy that the Gospel of John was addressed. The very first words are a flat denial of

41

that heresy and a ringing affirmation that God did indeed send his Son into the world and into the flesh. He called Jesus "the Word made flesh." (See John 1:1-14.)

An Adulterated Teaching

The heresy of *dualism*—which separated the spiritual from the physical world—was in direct contradiction to much of Christ's teaching, and especially to the belief in physical healing. The church of that day actually began to teach that God *sends* physical suffering in order to bring us spiritual lessons, that sickness was sometimes a participation in the sufferings of Christ, and that the Christian way was to surrender to the will of God. In the New Testament, anointing with oil was for the *healing* of the body, but it later became anointing for *death* or "extreme unction." The whole view of life had changed and suffering was seen in different light. Francis MacNutt makes this point most emphatically, then goes on to observe that now, once again, the practice of healing is being reestablished in the Catholic church and that the anointing of the sick for healing is again being observed.[2]

Other expressions of this dualistic belief and contempt for body led to monasticism or *asceticism*—the withdrawal from the world and all its evils to live an isolated life in meditation and prayer. Living conditions in the monastery were extremely austere and often there was self-punishment of various kinds. If you read the mystic writers of the medieval church you will find a great many references to the practice of self-abnegation and mortification. Obviously, there is a biblical teaching of self-denial—but not of self-hate! In any case, belief in healing was not fostered in such an atmosphere of rejection of material things and contempt for the body.

Martin Luther and other reformers reacted against such teaching, but the doctrine and practice of healing did not really come into its own at that time. Too much of the old viewpoint prevailed, and indeed still does.

The Puritans in the early days of America largely rejected the body and material things, scorning all pleasures and delights of the flesh. Even while they vigorously exploited the land and extracted the natural resources from it, they practiced, for the most part, a rather austere way of life which reflected their disdain for the "flesh."

Healing as the Purview of Science

With the development of science and technology, more and more ministry was possible to the body. Increasingly people turned to medicine, then to psychiatry, and so on. Hospitals sprang up for the care of both body and mind. The idea of divine healing tended to be relegated to certain "fundamentalist" religious groups and to "healers" who were sometimes suspect. The majority of Christians practically ignored the privilege of healing as taught in the Bible and practiced by Jesus and his early followers. As a matter of fact, those who believed in healing often were considered extreme and fanatical.

This is not to say that what medical science has done is contrary to the Bible—simply that in our dependence on science alone we have not really lived up to our privileges as Christians. There are many fine Christian physicians who would support the idea of trusting God for healing, though presumably they would urge us to live in harmony with nature's laws and to do all we can for ourselves. There is no basic contradiction between science and faith. Beyond what medicine can do, the laws of God still are operative.

Two major ideas, then, have tended to separate the physical from the spiritual: (1) the rejection of the body and all material things as less than good, and (2) the growing belief that the care of the body is the exclusive purview of science. One wonders how much sickness arises from a kind of self-condemnation and contempt for the body. Many conscientious Christians are confused at this point. They never have learned to love life or to rejoice in nature and its gifts. The body is to be kept in subjection, of course; but it is indeed God's gift to us.

Healing in the Church of God

Around the latter 1870s and the early 1880s the movement we know as the Church of God came into being in a spontaneous sort of way—people in various places who felt the need for greater spiritual liberty rejected the prevailing religious formalism and claimed full spiritual liberty on the basis of the Scripture. It was natural that, as the early leaders turned to earnest study of the Scriptures, the doctrine of divine physical healing would be stressed. While D. S. Warner, the movement's most noted early leader, was not a healing specialist, healing was a normal part of his teaching.

Of all the names associated with healing in the Church of God, that of Enoch E. Byrum was most notable. He was a man powerfully used of God, traveling widely and writing rather voluminously. His first major written work, *Divine Healing for Soul and Body,* was published in 1892. He stressed healing as part of the "evening light" and all the gifts of the Spirit as normal in the Church. Generally, Byrum discouraged the use of medicine, though he saw the value of setting broken bones and other such procedures. His second book, *The Great Physician–His Power to Heal* appeared in 1899. In 1919 *Miracles and Healing* came off the Gospel Trumpet Company press, and in 1928 his *Life Experiences* shared with thousands some of the remarkable healing experiences he had witnessed.

J. W. Byers' book, *The Grace of Healing,* came out about the same time as Byrum's second book in 1899. Byers saw healing as one of the "restored" blessings and gifts to the Church, as part of God's covenant with Israel, and very much a part of Jesus' ministry. He discounted the value of medicine and advised people to "abandon" it. He saw physical and spiritual sickness as being deeply related. He also emphasized the importance of proper care of the body by diet, exercise, and so forth. Byers also was a man of faith.

Other names associated with healing in the Church of God were J. Grant Anderson, whose *Divine Healing* was

44

published in 1926; E. H. Ahrendt, whose *Healing for All* appeared in 1931; and O. L. Yerty, whose *Christ the Master of All Diseases* came out in 1938. Anderson was typically moderate and tender in his approach, stressing good physical habits and a positive faith in God. Ahrendt himself had much sickness and shared insights which came out of his own experience. Yerty was an evangelist and wrote as he spoke—affirmatively and with emphasis on the promises. There were many others too numerous to mention.

The Church of God had no "corner" on healing. A growing number of independent evangelists emphasized it, some rather specializing in it—F. F. Bosworth and Aimee Semple McPherson, for instance. With a different emphasis there were such leaders as Sutherland Bonnell, Agnes Sanford, and Albert Edward Day. These are only a few examples. Divine healing was coming into its own.

Some Observations

A perusal of writings mentioned above leads to some observations which may bring the major teaching of the Church of God into some focus:

1. Healing is rooted solidly in the Scripture, both Old and New Testaments.

2. It is seen as part of God's plan of redemption with ample provision made.

3. Sickness is evil, a work of Satan, overcome by Christ.

4. It is best to trust God completely and not resort to medicines. (Especially does this appear in earlier writings.)

5. The teaching on healing is given support by many testimonies from experience.

6. The wholeness of the person is emphasized.

7. There is only vague awareness of psychological factors. (Psychology was still a very young and inexact science at that time.)

8. There is a surprising lack of emphasis on healing as taking place in the fellowship of caring persons, and of *united* prayer on behalf of the sick. One would have expected more of this in a group where so much stress was placed upon Christian unity and fellowship.

For Discussion

1. We have stressed the difference between the "holistic" view of life and the "dualistic" view. Why is this important in the consideration of physical healing?

2. Look within your own mind: How much have you "rejected" your body? Do you look upon your body as the temple of the Spirit? or its prison? What difference does it make?

3. How do you feel when you assess the teaching and practice of healing as you have experienced or observed it?

4. If you have been prayed for in the hope of being healed, how did you sense the involvement and care of your fellow Christians? Do you feel we have a real caring concern for one another? Share your experiences.

[1]*The Healing Ministry in the Church* (Richmond, Va.: John Knox Press), pp. 36-39.

[2]*Healing* (Notre Dame, Inc.: Ava Maria Press, 1974), p. 9. Dr. MacNutt, a priest in the Roman Catholic church, is probably its leading proponent of divine healing.

Chapter 6

Healing and Our Deeper Nature

FAR FROM LIFE'S being separated into two parts—
physical and spiritual—we now know better than ever that
it is one . . . that the physical, the emotional, and the
spiritual are dynamically interdependent and intertwining.
Even the universe itself is no longer conceived of as a machine, with the "spiritual" being only a romantic notion of
certain starry-eyed people. Developments in physics and
other sciences blast that idea.

As we have observed, the Bible gives a holistic view of
creation, of life, and of human nature. After a long circu-
itous route our society now returning to a new appreciation
for its wisdom on this point.

Psychoanalysis Teaches Us

A new view of humanity emerged in the scientific world
with the monumental work of Sigmund Freud (1856-1939),
the Austrian neurologist and founder of psychoanalysis. He
probed into the deeper nature of the human mind—the
subconscious—and found a very powerful relationship between that and human conduct, between deep feelings and
physical ailments. Following Freud many other astute
thinkers and researchers added to and amplified his

findings. This is not the place to explore all that. But it is important for us to recognize the revolutionary impact which psychoanalysis has had on our modern thinking.

Psychiatry unites the disciplines and skills of medicine with the treatment of emotional and mental disorders. In recent years this profession has abounded in both usefulness and prestige. Counselors of various disciplines try to relate their helping ministry to the insights of psychology. Pastors increasingly are studying the field in depth and many are taking clinical training to better prepare for their counseling work. Millions of people go to professional counselors every week in the hope of better understanding themselves and of finding relief from mental and emotional anguish.

And there is still a great unmet need. Estimates indicate that a high percentage of people who are in general hospitals (to say nothing of mental hospitals) are there because of mentally or emotionally induced illness. Psychosomatic (mind-body) illnesses abound, perhaps because of the stresses of modern life—but more likely because of the lack of the acceptance of God's love and the failure to live up to what is known to be right and true.

The Wisdom of the Bible

Revealing, as it does, the true nature of mankind as well as the will of God, it is not strange that the Bible takes account of our deeper nature. Long centuries before Sigmund Freud was born, the Scripture said, "Out of the heart are the issues of life" (Prov. 4:23). "As [a person] thinketh in his heart so is he" (Prov. 23:7). The Bible portrays the human being as made from the ground, but with the breath of God breathed in. One is a living being, a living *soul*. The word used in Genesis 2:7 means "spirit," but it is not the same word as used in reference to God, the eternal Spirit. The human spirit is derived, created. The Spirit of God is Creator.

48

The history of Israel is replete with instances where the Eternal Spirit speaks to the spirits of human beings. God spoke to Adam and Eve, to Noah, to Abraham, to Isaac, and to Jacob. He spoke through the psalmist and through the prophets. Most of all he spoke through Jesus Christ, "the Word made flesh." He spoke through the Apostles and the first-century Christians, sometimes in an astonishing way. The Bible declares human beings to be spiritual beings with physical bodies which are intended to be "temples" of the Spirit of God. In this respect, the findings of psychology are only a rediscovery of what always has been recognized in the Judeo-Christian teaching and experience.

Some Causes of Illness

The study of deeper causes of illness is a major undertaking. Fortunately qualified people in the field have given this issue responsible attention. One of the earlier scholars to do this was Dr. Leslie Weatherhead of England who—as a Christian, a clergyman, and a skillful counselor—brought unusual wisdom to the task. His sizeable volume entitled *Psychology, Religion, and Health** substantially changed the thinking of many Christian leaders. He devoted considerable attention to "causative" factors of illness, such as guilt and the deprivation of love. Then he proceeded to point out the great healing values in faith, love, confession, and worship. Stressing the importance of combining the insights and skills of psychotherapy with the powerful affirmations of the Christian faith, he pointed the way to a dynamic interaction and teamwork which can offer healing and wholeness to many.

Not all sickness comes from emotional problems, but much of it does—more than we like to admit. We who have been taught holiness have been prone to pretend that we have no problems, that all our questions have been answered, all our doubts have been expunged, and all our temptations have been put in the past forever. There isn't much room left for confession, for real honesty about ourselves. We tend to "put our best foot forward," to wear a righteous mask and play a sanctimonious role, for if we open up and reveal our real needs we may be rejected. This must be challenged. Honesty and openness are necessary to healing. We may sometimes be seeking physical healing when the deep need, the real need, is for spiritual healing. Our sins are not always the things we do. They may be what we think and feel. Jesus had much more to say about the sins of the spirit than about sins of the flesh.

Cleansing in the Fellowship

Could the Apostle James have had some of these sins of the spirit in mind when he enjoined the people to "confess your faults [some translations say 'sins'] one to another, and pray for one another, that ye may be healed" (5:16). It's hard to believe that he meant the confession of some juicy scandal, because such a confession would probably create more barriers than it would remove. And confession is intended to *remove* barriers, to open the way for the sharing of burdens, and to establish a unity of spirit. Sins of the spirit are the real barriers. Jealousy, malice, judgmental attitudes, criticism, envy, guile, pretense, and anything else unchristian or false will block the flow of spiritual energies in the individual person and in the group. We cannot really pray for one another and bear one another's burdens until there is open-hearted candor and honesty.

Note that this is supposed to take place in a fellowship of caring love. It is not something perfunctory or ritualistic or ceremonial. It is vital and life-sharing—in the love and life of Christ. When you observe some perfunctory healing services, you can see why we have no more real healing experiences. There often is only a kind of passing glance at the need, with little intercession or deep concern, little uniting in focused faith. Healing, therefore, must be considered in the light of the whole person with both physical and spiritual needs, and in the context of the caring fellowship of Christian brothers and sisters.

Confession as it apparently was practiced in the early church with its loving fellowship gradually was lost (maybe because of abuses, who knows?) Later it became the "confessional" where one confessed sins to the priest, and "sins" were things defined by the church as sins. Something precious was lost in the process, though we must admit there are some great values in confessing to one responsible person. (The modern psychiatrist or professional counselor has a kind of "confessional.")

"Let God Remold Your Minds"

The Apostle Paul was speaking to the deeper human needs when he wrote to the Romans (12:2): "Do not be conformed to this world but be transformed by the renewal of your mind, that you may prove what is the will of God, what is good and acceptable and perfect." The J. B. Phillips translation says, "Let God remold your minds from within. . . ." The intent is to let the Spirit of God search the deeper areas of the mind (the subconscious) and change the whole personality so that one will become a "transformed" person.

"Search me, O God," cried the psalmist, "and know my heart! Try me and know my thoughts! And see if there be any wicked way in me, and lead me in the way everlasting" (139:23-24). Obviously, the awareness of our deeper nature is nothing new!

To hammer on the "promises" and demand God's answer to our prayers is hardly the scriptural approach, then. The whole person is involved in the healing. Spiritual healing and physical healing are inextricably intertwined. The human being is a "corpo-mental" being. Body and mind interact powerfully. It is unthinkable to ignore the emotional and spiritual needs while demanding healing for the body. In the wisdom given by God, the early Christian leaders sensed this. It was said of Jesus that "he knew what was in man." Perhaps that is one reason why he could heal

51

so many people. His "methods" of healing were related to the deeper spiritual needs, too.

Healing of the Memories

In the past several years this term—"healing of the memories"—has come into fairly common use. Prayer has been offered and victories claimed for some who suffered from spiritual wounds, often in early life. This has been preceded by confession and sharing of the hurts—that is, so far as they were consciously recognized by the individual. Often there has been a lack of love in the parental home, or even hostility and abuse. To yield to the love of God and to loving persons, and to share the faith of a caring group can be a healing experience. In a conference a lady suddenly exclaimed with surprise, "I'm healed!" Who knows what sublime interaction can take place in a loving, caring, believing group where God's promises are claimed?

Inhibitions, fears, hostilities, and barriers hinder the flowing of spiritual energies. Stress, strain, and defensiveness can close a whole personality in upon itself, for the very barriers one raises in self-defense become the bars of his or her own prison. Healing comes as one realizes the love of others and the love of God. As sunshine warms and heals the body, so love warms and heals the spirit.

Levels of Confession

Some things probably should be confessed to God alone. Only with him can one let down *every* defense, for only in him is perfect unconditional love. This can and should be done.

Furthermore, for anyone who wishes to grow and mature, confession should be a continuous exercise. To turn yourself "inside out" with full awareness of God's love is a cleansing, healing experience.

But there is great value in finding an earthly counterpart to divine love. The fellowship of Christians ought to be that—and to a certain extent it is. But generally there are people who are not "unconditional" enough in their love or mature enough in their understanding to handle some confessions responsibly or confidentially, so wisdom is needed in this confession business.

There is a very important place for the Christian counselor with sound training who can bring psychological insights and Christian compassion together. Only eternity will reveal the good that has been done by such professional persons and by wise Christian pastors.

There is a vast ministry of "loving listening" to be done by ordinary people who have compassion enough to hear a person through without contesting for the "floor." Untold loneliness and anguish could be relieved if such a ministry of compassionate listening could take the place of judgmental, critical attitudes.

Physical healing is very closely tied in with the deeper nature. When more attention is given to such emotional and spiritual needs, more physical healing will take place.

For Discussion

1. Search your own mind for a moment. Do you find there some hurts and wounds which may be related to illness? How do you see yourself—as a *whole* person or as a person inwardly troubled?

2. What do you really believe about confession? Do you feel that you have a sound view of it? To what extent do you practice confession? To whom do you confess?

3. What is the role of the pastor in relation to the deeper hurts and needs? in relation to confession? How important is it for a pastor to have training in counseling?

4. Explore the meaning of Romans 12:2. Read it in different translations and discuss it. Do we dare to follow its instruction?

*Leslie D. Weatherhead, *Psychology, Religion, and Health* (Nashville: Abingdon Press, 1952).

Personal Notes

Chapter 7

Healing and the Miraculous

MODERN PEOPLE do not take readily to the idea of *miracles*—except, of course, as the word pertains to the accomplishments of medical science or to "miracle drugs." There, the reference is clearly to knowledge of nature's laws rather than to the transcendence of those laws.

The word *miracle* means an effect or an extraordinary event in the physical sense which surpasses all known natural powers or laws and so is attributed to a supernatural cause. It is an event or happening which is so far beyond human understanding that we say it is the action of some higher power. But is there a "higher power"? That's the nub of the question. How do we view life and creation? Here we are again with our recurring theme. If you see the universe as a machine, the idea of miracles would seem to be ridiculous. If you see the physical and material as all evil and far separated from the spiritual, it will appear incongruous. But if, with the biblical view, you believe in God who is Spirit filling the whole universe with himself and his power, then the idea of a miracle begins to make sense.

Philosophy and Mentality

Philosophically, during the nineteenth century the human being was regarded by science almost altogether in its material aspect. The body was the object of all sorts of scientific investigations which, we must admit, were very useful but which tended to exclude all other elements of the human personality. Medicine was primarily—even almost exclusively—centered on the physical. As we have pointed out before, it was not until the early twentieth century that the mental and emotional part of the human being was more fully appreciated.

Even the early psychology was largely a study in reactions, of stimulus and response, rather than the dynamics of personality. The emphasis has changed gradually so that now there is a keen awareness of the human being as much more complex. There has been a dawning realization of the importance of the subconscious, and a growing sense that the human psyche reaches out, touching a universal consciousness that holds both mystery and challenge. Now the growing edge of research seems to be in the direction of extrasensory perception (ESP) and the mystical. What does all this say to us? We are not very sure what all it is saying, but we are pretty sure that human beings do have a mystical, spiritual nature that reaches out far beyond the little space they take up on the earth.

A hundred years ago the world view was more mechanical than it is now. But it could hardly have been more mechanical and materialistic in *mentality* than now. That is to say, these days the patterns of thinking, the interests and priorities, are predominantly centered on the world of the physical senses. Thousands of Christians profess to believe in God and in spiritual things but they live by monetary values and their dependence is on material things. The Apostle Paul was talking about our mentality when he wrote to the Romans: "To set the mind on the flesh is death, but to set the mind on the Spirit is life and peace. For the mind that is set on the flesh is hostile to God; it does not submit to God's law, indeed it cannot . . ." (8:6-7). For Christians who read this, the real question is what gets our attention. To profess faith in God and spiritual values is not enough. If miracles and healing are to be ours, we must

56

have more than a tentatively-held and little-attended theoretical faith.

The Nature of Miracles

At one time a miracle was believed to be a violation of the laws of nature—or at least a suspension of those laws. In one way or another it was thought to be an interference with the natural order of creation. Now it is seen more as a revelation of power of which the origin is not in the laws of nature *as known to us*—in God the Creator who may use laws *unknown* to us. Nature itself could not produce a miracle.

How would a man have felt, say, in the very early days of the airplane, if he had never heard or read about its invention? He might look up into the bright sky, surprised by the noise of an engine, to see for the first time in his life an object that defied the law of gravity as he had known and experienced it. To him it would be a miracle! Everything in his experience would demand that it fall to the earth. But to his son who would go to college and learn the principles of aerodynamics, it would be explainable, though maybe still a bit awe-inspiring.

Our consideration must go beyond that, however. If we study the miracles which Jesus performed, we are driven to the conclusion that he employed spiritual laws and tapped a spiritual power. His own claim was that a *divine* power was brought into operation through him.

If that is true, would such spiritual laws be contradictory to nature's laws? Would not the God of the universe be the God of all laws both physical and spiritual? Can we imagine an immutable, unchanging, eternal God being self-contradictory or capricious? If this is indeed his creation, then it would be one harmonious whole, wouldn't it? God is indeed all powerful and unlimited, but is he not necessarily limited *by his own nature*? If he is a God of law and order, would he be so capricious as to violate his own nature and the laws of his creation?

It would seem more reasonable to think that when Jesus performed miracles it was by the operation of spiritual laws which *transcend* rather than violate physical laws. If one does believe in the reality of God as Spirit and the validity of spiritual laws, then the ministry of Jesus takes on the significance of divine lordship over all of life. And that is what he claimed: "All power is given unto me in heaven and in earth" (Matt. 28:18).

Miracles as "Signs"

The Apostle John, who probably was closer to Jesus than any other person, saw his miracles in a special light and with special meaning. He referred to them as "signs," which meant that they were astounding happenings which *pointed beyond themselves*—events with tremendous spiritual significance. Such a "sign" was a window fronting eternity, a clue to eternal, infinite meanings. Christ's miracles of love were God's object lessons in power and majesty and dominion.

Anyone who has experienced a miracle knows this to be true. It is an experience of God and his power. Life can never be quite the same anymore. The congregation that lives among miracles is one that people seek, for they seek to experience God. But it must be authentic. Simulated happenings or false claims will be an experience, not of God, but of deception. Christians must report what is actually true. Pretensions militate against the true experience and witness.

Miracles and C. S. Lewis

More than thirty years ago C. S. Lewis, the noted English author and teacher, wrote a book entitled *Miracles.** It was, and still is, one of the most responsible treatments of this subject by a leading thinker. It was a very cogent and snugly-reasoned argument insisting on the validity of miracles. Briefly summarized, his position was that—instead of being the violation of the laws of nature and of the body—a miracle is more like the speeding up of the processes of nature. A remarkable healing, for instance, would be the speeding up of the natural healing process. Or it might be the short-cutting of the natural process.

Some of the miracles of Jesus were apparently instantaneous; some were gradual, and the people "began to mend from that hour." Who knows what sublime interplay there was of physical and spiritual laws (if they can be thought of separately), and what changes in the physical process were effected? We know that positive attitudes of love, joy, faith, and optimism are very influential in physical recovery. Fear, worry, hostility, and pessimism slow down the healing process of nature. Positive faith in God and his power to heal makes a lot of sense, even from the viewpoint of our limited human understanding. If we can believe in the reality of the spiritual and in God who is Spirit; if we can believe that we human beings have a spiritual nature created by God; and if we can believe—as we surely must—that there is a deep and dynamic interplay of physical and spiritual forces within the human being and body, then how can we deny the reality of miracles?

And we are now just on the edge, the threshhold, of understanding this vast field of experience!

The Grand Miracle

Let us pursue C. S. Lewis just a little farther to the bright center of his thought. He believed that the incarnation of God in Jesus Christ was the "grand miracle" and the key to our understanding of the whole plan of creation itself. Christ was the union of God and nature, the influx of the spiritual into the physical. As John put it in the fourth Gospel, he was "the Word made flesh."

Suppose, Lewis said, that we have some parts of the manuscript for a novel. Then someone brings us a newly-discovered piece of manuscript saying, "This is the missing part of the work. This is the chapter on which the whole plot of the novel really turns." Our job, he said, would be to see whether the new passage would actually illuminate all the parts and pull them together in one harmonious whole. If it were genuine, then each reading would find it settling down very much at home and enhancing every part. That, Lewis says, is what the incarnation does to integrate and unify the whole meaning of creation. This gives tremendous significance to Jesus' words, "I am the way, the truth, and the life." That's what John saw. That's why he argued so strongly against falsely separating the physical and the spiritual realms. The Spirit of God had come into human flesh. It was no less than God's Son who walked in human sandals.

The Apostle Paul insisted that, in Jesus Christ, God would restore the whole creation to wholeness and harmony (see Colossians 1). He is the "chapter" upon which the whole plot turns. He illumines all other parts. Seek first his kingdom and everything else will be "added," or fall into place.

The virgin birth and the Resurrection, with all Christ's miracles and his miraculous life, are the divine event, the "grand miracle."

The Resurrection Crucial

The Resurrection of Jesus Christ was the supreme miracle. It was by far the most astounding reality and the most electrifying principle of the early church. This was related to miracles and new life most explicitly by Paul, who wrote to the Romans (8:11): "If the Spirit of him who raised Jesus from the dead dwells in you, he who raised Christ Jesus from the dead will give life to your mortal bodies also through his Spirit which dwells in you." Resurrection power! That was the key to the miracles seen in the early church.

Much has been said about "the power of mind over matter." This is not the place or time to examine that, but any one of us knows from experience something of the mind's influence over feelings. What about the power of Spirit over matter? the power of God over matter? The incarnation teaches us that the Eternal has invaded time, the Spirit has entered into human life. As Lewis said, "The union between God and Nature, in the Person of Christ, admits no divorce." It is time for Christians to halt the "divorce proceedings" and recognize the "grand miracle." Only so will they be alive to miraculous power.

For Discussion

1. Do you really believe in miracles? What do you believe *about* miracles? What is a miracle? Have you ever witnessed a miracle or experienced one? Take a response in your group—how many have seen a miracle?

2. Whatever you may think *about* miracles, what is your mentality? Does your frame of thinking and your scale of values permit miracles? What is the reason we don't experience more of divine power?

3. In your discussion, do not settle on the theoretical alone. What do you believe—actually, down deep?

4. Do you know anybody who seems to have the "gift of miracles," as spoken of in 1 Corinthians 12, or the "gift of healing"? Are we to take these "gifts" seriously in this modern day?

*C. S. Lewis, *Miracles* (New York: The Macmillan Company, 1947).

Personal Notes

Chapter 8

Healing in the Caring Fellowship

PERHAPS we do not experience more miracles and healings in these days because we think of each individual as being solely responsible to believe God's promise and get the answer to prayer. "According to your faith be it unto you," we often say glibly—and almost with a note of demand. That places the full responsibility on the sick one who, in a weakened and discouraged condition, may be wavering in faith. That is precisely the time when the supporting faith and love of fellow Christians is needed.

Often the greatest confidence a weakened person has is a belief in the prayers of trusted friends. To be surrounded by those whom we love and trust, and to be aware that they are uniting their faith for us, is a powerful stimulus to our personal faith.

The Setting for Healing

We tend to miss the corporateness in the Church as seen in the New Testament. For one thing, we think of the Church mostly as organization rather than as dynamic relationships. We think of it as a collection of individuals rather than as a people whose lives have flowed together in the life of Christ.

But it seems the Lord deals with his people primarily as a body. The Holy Spirit led the early Christians as they prayerfully counseled together. According to Paul, every individual was called to Christian vocation, but each one was called to be *part of the called company* (see Ephesians 4). Each was called to a living hope, but it was "the one hope" which united them in the common venture. Each was to receive some gift of the Spirit; but the gift was really a gift to the Church, to be exercised for the edification of the whole body of believers. It is the Church as a body, more than the individual as a person, that reveals the ministry of the Holy Spirit.

So it was that prayer for healing was to be done in the fellowship of believers. They were to "bear one another's burdens and thus fulfill the law of Christ" (Gal. 6:2). They were to have a mutual concern for one another. The sick one was to "call for the elders of the church," and this most likely took place normally as the believers were assembled together. They were to confess their faults to one another and pray for one another for healing in the fellowship of love.

The setting probably was in the informal group where they were "breaking bread from house to house" and where they ate together "with gladness and singleness of heart." Some have called that early form of worship the "love feast." They shared their food and their experiences. They observed the Lord's Supper together, claiming the presence of the risen Christ himself. It was very likely in that kind of a setting where the sick would ask the elders of the group to pray for them—where the whole company of believers would be united in love and faith.

United prayer was a significant part of this. Jesus had said that when even two *agreed* upon one thing, their prayer would be answered. That is united, focused, believing prayer.

The Law of Love Was Basic

Jesus clearly taught that love must be aggressive, caring, and positive, seeking out the need. "As you would that men should do unto you, do ye even so to them." That's positive caring. The principle had been stated in the negative many times, even in different countries and cultures—"Do not do unto others what you would not want them to do unto you." That simply says we must not do harm to others. But Jesus said we should "do" to others. That means the person who is helpless and sick, suffering and in need, will be the object of our care and concern.

This was true in Jesus' own life. As we have already noted, Jesus gravitated to the unlovely, the sick, the rejected, the lost, and the lonely. His love was positive and incisive. "If one member suffers," said Paul to the Corinthians, "all suffer together; if one member is honored, all rejoice together" (1 Cor. 12:26). The early Christians were to "weep with those who weep and rejoice with those who rejoice." The prime characteristic of the Church, according to Jesus, was to be the manifest love and care they had for one another. "By this shall all men know . . ."

In the Christian sense, love has been defined as "intelligent moral concern." It is not "free love" or mere sentiment. It is mutual care and compassion. At its best it is *unconditional*. Jesus said, "A new commandment I give to you, that you love one another; even as I have loved you, that you also love one another" (John 13:34). That is unconditional love. It is the very heart of true fellowship.

The Spirit of Openness

It is in the atmosphere of such love and trust that a person can be open, honest, and candid. "Confess your faults one to another . . ." says James 5:16. But that is impossible in an atmosphere of suspicion or criticism. James says that such openness is the condition for healing. There can be no freedom of the spirit until the barriers of fear and distrust are removed. Renewal is preceded by repentance, and healing is often preceded by confession. Perhaps if there were more honest, open confessions of needs, fears, and faults, there would be more healings.

Metals which would never unite at low temperature can be fused together at high temperature. They can even be melted together into an inseparable unit so that the resulting product is stronger than any of the constituent metals. So it could be said of the early followers of Jesus. The personalities of those disciples were very different. It was a motley group indeed—some fishermen, a tax collector, a revolutionary, and others who had little in common—but they were fused into a unity in the furnace of deep fellowship in Christ. That in itself was a miracle. More of this spiritual heat is needed if barriers are to be melted away and real healing power released.

Whatever power there was in that early fellowship is inherent in the person and power of Christ who was central and preeminent among them. That is what they believed. They had personally known and walked with the Christ who lived on a higher spiritual plane than we ordinary human beings can know. They knew that spiritual energies of immense power were at his disposal, and they claimed that kind of power in his name. They could call into operation the spiritual laws, in his name. But to do this, their selfish defenses and the barriers that kept each in isolation had to yield to oneness in Christ. And that is just the meaning of fellowship as they spoke of it—*Koinonia*—it was their life-sharing relationship in the life of Christ. Divine healing takes place best in a fellowship which transcends individual action and faith. The power of Christ is most real in the Body of Christ, the Church.

Healing, a Ministry of the Church

There is no need for making a false distinction between healing as a personal ministry and healing as a ministry of the Church. Yet there often has been confusion at this point. The "healer" so often has been seen as a specialist with an independent ministry. We should recognize that, in the New Testament, healing had its expression primarily in the Body of Christ, the Church.

For one thing, as we have said, every gift of the Spirit is a gift to the Body of Christ and is to be exercised for the edification and blessing of all the believers. "Now there are varieties of gifts," says 1 Corinthians 12:4-7, "but the same Spirit, and there are varieties of services, but the same Lord; and there are varieties of working, but it is the same God who inspires them all in every one. To each is given the manifestation of the Spirit for the common good." Each gift is to be exercised as a part of the ministry of the Church, not to secure a personal following.

The purpose is vital! For one thing, the Spirit's fruits will be conserved and extended by the ministry of the whole body of believers, while benefits of the individual operation—the tangential movement—will largely be lost. For another thing, every person—no matter how sincere or gifted—needs the guidance, the correction, and the support of the whole body.

The more one's work proves helpful and valuable, the more it draws the attention to the person as one especially chosen by God. One might say again and again that all power comes from God and that one's witness is only in the name of Christ; but the attention of those to whom one ministers is nonetheless directed toward that person as a *special* servant of God. The result often is a personality cult. And who is able then to escape from the feeling of power arising out of perpetual adoration? This leaves the door open to a false self-image and grandiose notions about oneself. The true servant of God will strenuously *resist* such an individualistic course, and carefully avoid allowing such attention to be personal. When any person, regardless of the gifts possessed, becomes the issue—with people saying, "I am of Paul" or "I am of Apollos"—then that person is guilty of dividing the people of God, either deliberately or by default. It is so easy then for one's followers to take the next step in the process and brand the Church as less than spiritual and only the special one and the cult as really spiritual.

This can be avoided and the Holy Spirit's work preserved by working, as the New Testament clearly teaches, in the fellowship of believers, the Body of Christ, the Church.

The Gift of Healing

In this context, let us clearly recognize the validity of the gift of healing as given by the Holy Spirit. Certainly God does use certain persons, giving them real gifts of service. Healing is one of them, though not the only one. This has been true across the years. There are some who have had a memorable and lasting ministry, blessing many. Their very presence has encouraged faith. Their well-known compassion has warmed and moved many hearts. Their quiet faith in God has been used in sometimes very remarkable ways. And their ministry continues long after their active careers come to a close. We can thank God for them, and for all who have humbly exercised the gifts of the Spirit in loving service.

The gifts of the Spirit are encouraged and experienced, however, only by positive teaching and a dynamic spiritual fellowship. There are some congregations where there is even discouragement of healing and cynicism. What we say here presupposes a condition of spiritual vitality and Christian compassion. Healings are not likely to take place in a cold, formal atmosphere or under the pastoral leadership of pseudo-sophistication. If a congregation is largely backslidden at heart, divine healing will sound unrealistic. But for a people deeply committed to God and to the validity of scriptural teaching, it will be like the warm light of the sun on a dark and gloomy day. When we take the reality of healing seriously, there will be gifts of healing among us.

Barriers to Healing

While there may have been some exceptions to what we shall say now, the truth is that barriers to fellowship become barriers to healing. To claim healing means to surrender oneself to God's love and to the love of his people, and those two directions of relationship go together. The person who cannot receive the love of fellow Christians will not likely be able to receive God's love either. The inability to receive and give love—to God and to other people—is basically an estrangement and alienation. The ability to do so brings one into living, vital, spiritual relationships.

But many of us have had the feeling that if people really knew us they wouldn't accept us, that we would be criticized, judged, and rejected. Probably nothing keeps us from the healing experience so much as to feel basically alone and unloved. A study of the gospel shows that the revelation of God's love for us will constitute the real foundation for a new life for that one who really received it. "In this is love, not that we loved God but that he loved us and sent his Son . . ." To receive—actually receive, personally—the unconditional love of God is basic to the new life.

And closely related to that is receiving the love of God's people. The loving fellowship is intended to be the earthly, human counterpart of God's love. As a matter of fact, many must experience the love of God through his people. That's divine love one can see and sense and realize.

Then let the Church be the loving fellowship God intended. When it is, healing will be a normal part of its ministry.

For Discussion

1. Is there, in your congregation, a spirit of openness and love which is conducive to healing? Evaluate this honestly.

2. Where and when do you customarily pray for the healing of the sick? Is it the best time and under the best conditions? How much focused, united prayer takes place?

3. Do you agree that the ministry of healing belongs in the fellowship of the Church? If so, how can it be strengthened, made more meaningful and effective?

4. Do you accept the idea that confession often is necessary to remove barriers and make healing possible? What fears do you have about confession in the Church?

Personal Notes

Chapter 9

Prayer for Healing

PRAYING for the sick ought never to be a perfunctory or superficial exercise. There is no magic attached to a certain ritual or ceremony. It is to be a vicarious experience in which those who are relatively well and of good spirit enter into the hurts and needs of the one who is suffering. It is to "bear one another's burdens and thus fulfill the law of Christ." It is to recognize the fact that the afflicted one is probably less able than usual to exercise faith on his or her own behalf. It is to "get under" the burden, to share that burden, to lift it up to the God of all love and power. It is to share with the often weakened and discouraged person the contagion of our faith, the lifting bouyancy of our love, and the affirmation of divine promise.

It is something near to crassness and mental cruelty to place the whole responsibility upon the sick person. "According to your faith be it unto you" we say. The sick one does indeed need to exercise faith, but the supporting faith of trusted Christian friends is needed. Sometimes the inference is made, "If you are not healed, it is because of some sin in your life." And that adds more condemnation and guilt. Often according to *our* faith the healing is given.

Discerning the Need

Prayer for the sick, with the anointing and laying on of

hands, often has been done too quickly, before the real need is sensed and before the afflicted one is prepared. Special counsel is sometimes needed. This is one of the reasons why the healing ministry belongs in the ministering congregation and with the leadership of a loving, wise pastor who normally will be in a position to pretty well know the need. It might be only a physical problem. It might be a physical-emotional problem. It might be an almost totally emotional or mental problem. It might arise out of conflict in the family. Whatever the problem, it will make a difference in how we pray. The true servant of God is called upon to help prepare a person for healing and to follow up with encouragement and comfort. The pastor and other Christian friends may well have a part in this ministry of preparation. Just to have the right kind of reading material—as well as guidance in using the Scriptures—and dwelling on the great promises will prepare a person for the anointing experience.

Fallacy of Superficial "Answers"

When a person has a deep and real problem, the glib, superficial answer can be very offensive. And all too often our unctious, platitudinous words are just that—largely because we have not *listened*, we have not sensed what the real heart cry is. Blessed indeed is the pastor who can listen with genuine attention and compassion. And blessed is the Christian who recognizes this as a major spiritual ministry. A large part of the preparation for a healing experience is the simple sharing of the real sense of need, not a quick assumption and a spurious "answer." We don't pray better largely because we don't even know what the problem is.

Divine healing calls for a better response on our part. It calls for identifying with the need and entering into the spirit of caring. Glenn Clark, a man powerfully used in prayer, used to say that when someone asked him to pray for a person he first learned all he could about that person and the need, entering into as complete a sense of identification as he could. Then when he felt the hurt in his own heart, he would lift that friend and himself up to God. When the burden lifted, he said, he knew his prayer had been answered. That is the vicarious principle in prayer. That's intercession. It is more than superficial, ready-made "answers." It is more than a ritual or ceremony carried out. It is burden sharing.

Anointing with Oil

Even under Jesus' ministry, when the disciples were sent out two by two, they "anointed with oil many that were sick and healed them" (Mark 6:13). While the Book of the Acts of the Apostles makes no reference to anointing with oil, we may safely assume that it took place, probably very frequently. In the Epistle of James (5:14-15) it seems to be assumed as a common and current practice in the Christian community, for the point is not labored. James simply said: "Is any among you sick? Let him call for the elders of the church, and let them pray over him, anointing him with oil in the name of the Lord; and the prayer of faith will save the sick man, and the Lord will raise him up; and if he has committed sins, he will be forgiven."

Anointing with oil was a visible symbol of the action of the Holy Spirit. It was used in Israel in the consecration of kings, prophets, and priests. It is the symbol of the Spirit of God which consecrates and enables the anointed person to fulfill a divinely appointed mission. It implies consecration also, and it is in keeping with the concept that one is beseeching God for wholeness of body, mind, and spirit. Healing is not necessarily the goal, but wholeness. Healing is the means by which the Lord renders one capable of serving more fully. Thus, for the most part, it is thought of as applying to people of the Christian community. There may be exceptions but anointing belongs among Christians.

The anointing is to be done by responsible, recognized leaders in the fellowship and is normally a communal act. On behalf of the concerned group the anointing is done and the whole group unites in prayer. Ordinarily the finger is wetted with oil from a vial and placed upon the forehead of the sick. Then prayer is offered.

73

Laying on of Hands

The laying on of hands is not something new. It has a long history. And this is understandable. There's something sacred and warm about the touch of compassion. This also was done in many sacred ceremonies. Ordination, for instance, was done by the laying on of hands of the recognized leaders on the candidate for ordination. It signifies contact, continuity, compassion, and confidence. Again, it is on behalf of the caring fellowship that we lay our hands upon the head, the forehead, or the shoulders and neck, praying the prayer of faith. It is not so much a ritual or ceremony as it is the act of conveying our compassion and caring.

The laying on of hands is an act of worship. In that act God comes near to the afflicted one as he is represented by the body of believers. The sick one responds to God. The touch of the "elder" is a symbol of divine love coming into the broken body and life. It is God's love and the sick one's response. It represents a uniting or reuniting with God. Thus there is discharged into the brokenness of the sick one the spiritual energy that comes from God alone. Illness is a by-product of the disunity from God. The laying on of hands signifies the fresh-born unity with God.

Those who are recognized leaders often feel very deeply the need for the love and agreement of the total group. It really is a pretty awesome responsibility to thus minister in the name of Christ and his body, the Church.

United Faith

United prayer is not the same as the prayer of worship. It is different from any other kind of prayer. It has a specific, sharp focus on a particular need and concentrates all the compassion, the spiritual energy, and the faith of the group on one thing. Jesus was referring to this principle when he said, "Again I say to you, if two [even two!] of you agree on earth about anything they ask, it will be done for them by my Father in heaven'' (Matt. 18:19). The Authorized version says "as touching any thing." The emphasis is on a specific need rather than general needs. The text indicates concentration, persistence, and full agreement by the congregation. It is more than a passing glance at the need, and more than a casual mention.

A review of experiences of answered prayer would indicate that agreement is one of the common features of effective healing ministry. Even in the cases of lauded special "healers," the secret is in the prayer strength of others. It should say something about a pastor's need for prayer support among the believers.

In time past there were frequent instances when, before prayer was offered for the sick, anyone who did not believe would be asked to leave the room so as not to be a hindrance. Perhaps that would not be an inappropriate practice now. United prayer, in full agreement and faith, is vital. When prayer for the sick becomes perfunctory, the failures following upon it are further discouraging to faith.

Prayer by Proxy

There are times when the sick or troubled one is not present, perhaps is even many miles away. If there is a serious request for prayer, we sometimes pray for such a person by proxy. (While there probably is no instance of this given in the Scripture, it is true to the principle seen in the Scriptures.) We ask the one who makes the request, or the person in the group who knows the sick one best and who cares most deeply, to come as proxy for the sick. While that person fully identifies with the need and affliction of the sick one, we pray for the sick through him or her. This person takes the place of the sick one by vicarious identification. The greater the person's compassion, the better. And united faith can be better exercised by such practice.

Distance is no factor with God. Jesus healed people from

a great distance away. Experience teaches us that when the united prayer of faith is offered, some remarkable answers come.

Special Settings for Healing

Probably nothing simulates the setting and relationships experienced in the early church so much as the *small, face-to-face groups* which have become an increasingly vital force in the pilgrimage of many Christians. When a small group of people meet regularly over a period of time, sharing their needs, supporting one another, praying for one another, some deep relationships are established. It is in such an atmosphere of mutual care that the united prayer of compassion and faith most naturally takes place. That often is the best school of prayer—assuming, of course, proper guidance has been given and the relationships have been deep.

Another unique setting for united prayer is the *retreat,* where a group of people may set aside several days for spiritual and intellectual quest. It is a time of learning, of deep sharing, of counsel together, and of prayer for one another. The most authentic answers to prayer I have ever seen have been in such retreats. There is something about the deeper relationships which come only over a more sustained period of time that is most conducive to compassion for one another and to united faith. Lives are opened, confidence is established, and a trusting atmosphere, normally, is achieved.

Why do we not make more of *the Lord's Supper* as a time for healing? Presumably there, as at no other place and time, we are most united in the Spirit—or should be. If we claim the living presence of the Lord, can we not claim his healing power?

It is interesting to note that the Apostle Paul brings Communion and healing together. After warning the Corinthians against the abuse of Communion he condemns those who eat and drink without discernment and who bring reproach on that sacred privilege. "For any one who eats and drinks without discerning the body eats and drinks judgment upon himself. That is why many of you are weak and ill, and some have died" (1 Cor. 11:29-30).

If the health and wholeness of the body is connected with the perfect life of the Holy Spirit acting in it, then it would seem that at no point would there be a more likely setting for healing ministry than at the time of communion at the Lord's table. Some of the early Church leaders celebrated Holy Communion "for the remission of sins, for renewal of souls and bodies."

Continuing Support

Often when a person has experienced the prayer for healing and has put his or her trust in God, there are tests of faith to follow. As we shall see in the next chapter, there are disciplines of faith to be followed. But here let us stress the importance of the word of encouragement and affirmation to be given. The group, as well as the individual, has a significant concern. The battle of continual faith, also, is one to be waged by the whole body of believers.

In a word, we Christians stand together. We need one another. When one member of the body of Christ hurts, all the others hurt too. That's the way it is in a caring fellowship.

For Discussion

1. Should we change our practice of praying for the sick at the end of a public service? Is there a better setting for it? What kind of conditions would be most conducive to united faith?

2. What about preparation of the sick person before the anointing? What measures could we take to encourage faith on the part of others as well?

3. Is it proper for a person's need to be expressed audibly before the assembled group? What are the advantages in that? disadvantages?

4. Discuss what you feel is the pastor's part in preparation. Should the pastor counsel with the sick one beforehand? Discuss these practical aspects of the healing experience.

Personal Notes

Chapter 10

Healing and Personal Faith

WHAT we have said about the caring, believing fellowship and its importance for healing does not obviate the need for personal faith in God. It is true that often we need the support of our Christian brothers and sisters; but in some degree the afflicted person has to accept personal responsibility and believe the promise of God for personal healing. After all, Jesus did say to the woman with a hemorrhage, "Your faith has made you well" (Matt. 9:22). And to the blind men he said, "According to your faith be it unto you." (v. 29). Yet when you examine the instances of Jesus' healings, it is difficult to see how some of those whom he healed could have had anything like a "normal" faith as we might think of it. There must have been something very powerful in his physical presence and in his reputation as the promised Messiah which inspired a simple faith. One is inspired to believe in the presence of a person of great faith.

The atmosphere of thinking was different then. There was less sophistication (or pseudo-sophistication!) than now. The people were probably more conditioned for simple faith. In any case, there always is the need for personal faith. But perhaps we should clarify what we mean by this.

What Kind of Faith?

Let us distinguish, first, between *faith* and *credulity*. Is faith only for simple, superstitious people? Is it, as a school boy said, "believing what you know isn't true?" Is faith for us in these days of science and education?

It is important that we see faith in its true light. It is not unreasonable; it goes beyond reason. It is not irrational; it goes beyond rational powers. Faith is basic reverence before God and the mystery of life. It is to seek understanding as far as the light of our reason can take us, but to stand bareheaded at the rim of that light recognizing the vast distance beyond that rim. In the context of our discussion here, faith is to recognize that there are physical and spiritual laws above and beyond our knowledge and that God, the Creator of all, is above all and "able to do exceeding, abundantly more than we can ask or think" (Eph. 3:20). It is a mistake to equate faith with superstition and credulity.

However, faith is simple, not sophisticated. No matter how much we may know (or think we know) there is need for the child-like, simple belief in God. Jesus placed great emphasis on this, even taking a little child into the circle of followers, saying, "Unless you turn and become like children, you will never enter the kingdom of heaven. Whoever humbles himself like this child, he is the greatest in the kingdom of heaven" (Matt. 18:2-4).

Faith is submissive, not manipulative. We don't storm the gates of heaven with our demands. God will be God in his own way. We do not inform him. We do not persuade him. We do not use him. We are to submit to him with confidence in his love for us and his will for our highest good. We do not bend him to our will; rather, we submit to his will and lay hold of his highest willingness. Submission and faith go together—and lead to wholeness. He heals in different ways. Trust him.

Faith has to be continuous, not sporadic. Many a healing experience is lost because we return to doubts and fears. The mind must be disciplined to cling persistently to the promises of God.

We do not speak of faith in faith. It must be faith in God, believing his promises. "With God all things are possible." The act of faith is a vital step, but the act must be made continuous. This is a personal responsibility. No one else can do it for us. They can encourage and affirm the promises to us; but often there is a battle of faith in our own hearts which no one else can win for us.

It helps to remember that our faith is placed in a Person, not in an idea. That Person is utterly reliable, unconditionally loving, and fully trustworthy. The faith of which we speak is simply believing his promises. That's where we take hold.

Surrender to Love

As I mentioned before, the deepest problem that many of us have is the inability to receive and to give love. Persons for whom we pray are likely to feel alone and put to the test of personal faith, wondering whether they can have enough faith and be healed to achieve the approval of the group. This produces a strain so that may hinder faith. Now, it is important for the fellowship that prays to be loving; but the persons for whom we pray need also to open their hearts to the love of God and of fellow Christians.

To do that can be a transforming experience spiritually. It can bring the inrushing realization of love. Many people never have experienced love in such a manner. To open the mind and heart fully—to accept, receive, and realize the love of God and of the people of God—is unforgettable! And it is a powerful stimulant to one's personal faith.

Thus, if a person can begin by believing in God's love and the love of caring people, the faith in God's willingness and power to heal will come quite naturally, especially if it has been preceded by openness, sharing of needs, and even confession. As Christian friends feel the need and enter into the person's struggles, there is greater compassion, more united prayer, and greater confidence in God's love.

81

It involves a proper self-love, too. This is to be taken in the sense used in the great two-fold commandment, "Love the Lord thy God . . . and thy neighbor *as thyself*" (Luke 10:27). Many people cannot accept themselves. They really hold themselves and their own bodies in contempt. It may well be that many people are sick because they hate their own bodies. God made us, soul and body. He loves us in our totality. It is impossible for a person to receive God's love if that person cannot love God's gift. Some of those who have wide experience in this field of divine healing counsel people to love the affected part of the body and accept with gratitude and joy even that as God's gift.

Forgive and Seek Forgiveness

Along with the promise of healing in James 5 is the promise of forgiveness. "The prayer of faith will save the sick man, and the Lord will raise him up; and if he has committed sins, he will be forgiven" (v. 15). It would seem that—inherent in the very experience of surrender to God's will—in the receiving of love and in the spirit of confession, we find the basic conditions for spiritual renewal. It would be incongruous to seek healing while holding grudges or defending inner guilts. The God "who forgiveth all thine iniquities, who healeth all thy diseases" will renew us physically and spiritually.

Love should bathe all of our relationships. We should give our forgiveness to any and all who have offended us. Forgiveness must be sought for our offenses against others. The slate is to be wiped clean. This ought to include deep personal hurts insofar as we are aware of them. Often people who have come for healing in one specific area have found that they were healed in other areas as well. Not always, but sometimes. We do not understand all that happens within the body and mind, but we do know that the promise of healing in body and soul is ours to claim when we meet the conditions.

It should be clear that divine healing ought to be considered—and experienced—in the larger context of spiritual relationships and wholeness. When it is, it takes on a new and beautiful dimension.

Sustained Attention

Whatever gets your attention eventually gets you. The kind of thoughts which occupy the mind will influence the whole mood and outlook. This is true, of course, in the short term. But it is even more true in the long pull. "Be not conformed . . . but transformed," said Paul, "by the renewing of your minds" (Rom. 12:2). Some people never will be healed because they simply will not exercise the self-discipline necessary to maintain positive attitudes and faith.

Perhaps some of these people, consciously or unconsciously, *want* to be sick. Jesus asked one man, "Do you want to be made whole?" (John 5:6). It's a question one might well ask before praying for the sick. "Do you really want to be well?" If not, it really is a mockery to pray for wholeness. Thus a basic responsibility rests upon the sick person. The lesson is to take God and his promise seriously, and not to take oneself too seriously. Look at the promises, not the symptoms. Anyway, if you begin with your problems, you will end with problems—and you will be a problem. It is the positive, continuous attention to God and his promises that becomes what one thinker called "the expulsive power of a new affection."

Continual Thanksgiving

Thanksgiving is the highest form of prayer, and faith. It is affirming, with gratitude. Experience teaches us that when we take the step of active faith, the best follow-up is one of thanking God for his own answer, in his own way, surrendering the whole need or problem into his care. One then is relieved of anxiety and stress. The mind is quieted. The emotions tend to be calm. That very fact is highly beneficial, even in the purely physical sense. The body functions at optimum efficiency when the mind is at ease and the heart is glad. As the saying goes, "A merry heart doeth good like a medicine."

As the Apostle Paul enjoined the people, "In everything give thanks." That has a way of lifting the whole problem or need up to a higher plane. Thank God even when symptoms may recur or in the midst of the problem. In everything give thanks—everything!

Visualize Wholeness

Imagination and visualization can project our real desires. *See* yourself whole. Fantasize a little about it. Let it dwell in your mind as a beautiful thing. Turn in at the gate of imagination and become childlike in faith. When you pray for somebody else use the same visualized faith.

What a powerful thing it is for a whole group of praying people to visualize a person whole and well and strong, and keep on with that practice. It is a powerful, supporting faith.

If the healing does not come right away, remember that some of the people Jesus healed did not get well instantly. Some "began to mend from that hour." In some ways this is the most rewarding kind of experience, for it is an unfolding one.

The writer of the Hebrew letter gave us good and practical counsel: "Therefore do not throw away your confidence, which has a great reward. For you have need of endurance, so that you may do the will of God and receive what is promised" (10:35-36).

The Witness to Healing

There are some who have taught that when you have received the anointing with oil with the laying on of hands, you are to claim healing at that moment as an accomplished fact. They say that if you have been sick in bed, you must get up, get dressed, and go about your work. When you meet people, they say, you should testify that you have been healed. It is only fair to say, however, that such claims may have brought reproach rather than witness. It is perfectly proper to say that you have put your trust in God for healing, but when describing your condition you had better tell the simple, plain truth—nothing more. Faith does not call for the sacrifice of integrity.

Authentic healings are a powerful testimony. To testify of authentic healing is glorifying to God. But false professions are a reproach, and spurious "testimonies" do more harm than good.

To summarize, the prayer for healing is most effective as a group experience, and the support of the fellowship is very meaningful as one fights the battle of faith. But it is the continuous sustaining personal faith that may well bring the reward.

For Discussion

1. Let someone in your group relate his or her experience in continuing faith. How was faith sustained? How was the battle won—or lost?

2. What can we say or do when another person is struggling through times of uncertainty? How can we help one another?

3. Some people have practiced certain disciplines to encourage and strengthen their faith. Share at this point. What has helped you most?

4. Have you ever been prayed for but not actually healed? How did you feel—embarrassed? guilty? criticized? Why?

Personal Notes

Chapter 11

Healing and Obedience to God's Laws

IT REALLY IS ridiculous to think that divine physical healing can come at our demand, regardless of how we live, how we think, and how we treat our bodies. It is equally untenable to think of healing as just some specific thing we call upon God to do for us—such as healing some particular ailment—while we withhold our beings from him and, in effect, refuse the wholeness he offers. Healing is to be thought of as wholeness restored, as harmony with God's laws of creation.

The human body is a marvelous thing given by God. It is his gift to us. Rejoice in it. Any trace of self-contempt and of shame are to be discarded. The body is to be the "temple" of the Holy Spirit. We are to present our bodies (with all their functions) as a "living sacrifice holy, and acceptable to God." All our faculties are to be given back to the Creator with gratitude and joy. Those faculties and functions are to be holy and acceptable to God, to be used as an act of worship. That instruction from Romans 12 is in full accord with the teachings of the Judeo-Christian faith.

Respect Physical Laws

How much suffering do people bring upon themselves?

You need only to look around you to see them soaking themselves with nicotine and alcohol, grossly overeating and overworking, disregarding the normal need for exercise and fresh air, and so on. When you stop to think about it, some people seem almost to be trying to destroy themselves.

And this, too often, is true of Christians. We are not too different from others in this respect. Sometimes, after disregarding nature's laws, people come to request prayer for their healing. Would we not avoid much sickness, and could we not have more faith for healing, if we paid more attention to the proper care of our bodies?

Some of our spiritual leaders have had much to say on this subject. It was very much a part of their teaching on the subject of healing, and properly so. They recognized that faith for healing had to be matched by obedience. Some were almost diet "buffs," and as they traveled about in evangelistic work, they often insisted on specially-prepared foods (much to the consternation of some of their hostesses!). It is not mere coincidence that those deeply devoted people who were so used by God in healing were also humble, obedient servants in observing his commands. They were careful students of the Scripture and they knew that divine healing could not be divorced from obedience to divine laws.

Hebrew Law Prescribed Physical Care

The Lord God was concerned about the physical care of his people. He promised that as long as they would obey his commandments he would be with them, bless them, and protect them. They were to be an uncontaminated people, free from the "abominations" of the pagan people around them. In a time of promiscuous moral relations and debauchery, they were to be a people of moral rectitude. This had to do not only with their morality and standards, but also with the prevention of disease and physical contamination.

Through the Levitical code, God gave them quite elaborate instructions as to what they might and might not eat. A careful reading of Leviticus 12-15 will reveal great care for the kinds of meat which were or were not permissible. And it is noteworthy that the instruction given in that long-ago age, centuries before the development of medical science and dietetics, is still valid. In recent years some of the investigations have shown that the Christian groups which have taken the Mosaic law seriously have a much lower incidence of certain dread diseases.

There also were laws governing sanitation and cleanliness. A careful examination will show that these were very important measures in that society and time for the prevention of infection and the spread of diseases then prevalent. There were measures for the containment of certain diseased persons, such as lepers—which we would call *quarantine*.

There were carefully drawn ceremonial laws to be followed in carrying out their worship by sacrifices, and other routines of daily life. These were necessary for sanitation and the protection of the people as well as expression of their devotion.

All this was because the Lord God cared about bodies as well as souls. It is in keeping with the whole concept that all of life is under his lordship. As he commanded them to keep a high ethical standard, to maintain justice in human relations, and to carry out religious worship, so he commanded them to care for their own bodies. It was a sacred obligation.

Greater Knowledge Today

With the development of modern science a revolution has taken place in our manner of life. Large hospitals can be seen in any significant city. Great medical centers have gained national and international reputation. Some of the most noted names in history have been of the medical profession. Eminent surgeons have performed unbelievable surgical operations. Dietetics has grown into a major study and the knowledge of vitamins and minerals (and calories!) is commonplace. Any knowledgable housewife and mother gives serious attention to balanced meals. Health food stores abound. And special diets are promoted by any number of specialists who claim the knowledge of most of our maladies.

This surely is not the place to expound on these things, but it is appropriate to emphasize the greater responsibility we have now to live wisely. There is no reason for ignorance and no excuse for irresponsibility.

With all that is known about the influence of our thinking and attitudes on physical health, surely the one who seeks healing will cooperate with God by keeping the right mental attitude. Who should be in a better position to have that positive attitude of faith, hope and joy than the Christian? Yet it often is distressing to see persons who are seeking healing continuing to think their dark, negative thoughts of doubt, fear, and foreboding. Christian healing comes with Christian attitudes.

Healing and Medical Science

Is there a contradiction between medical treatment and divine healing? between pills and prayers? Some very sincere and conscientious people have felt that there was, though not so much now as in earlier days. Actually, medical science often was suspect in the view of those who believed fervently in divine healing, not only in the sense that it was felt to be unnecessary, but also in the sense that medical science was felt to be incompetent and unreliable. Trust God alone, they said. To their way of thinking, to take medicine was not only a denial of faith, it was a contradiction of God's will. A few extremists went so far as to court disaster.

On the other hand, the tendency now among many Christian people is virtually to ignore divine healing and to rely altogether upon medical science. Some even sneer at the idea of divine healing. The tendency now is to take medicine, drugs, pain killers, sedatives, and all sorts of patent remedies—even to the point of being injurious to their health. So much for the extremists. There are two ditches, one on *each* side of the road.

If God is the author of all the laws of the universe, as he surely is, then do we have the right to make a distinction between the physical and the spiritual? Here we are right back to the same basic question. If all creation, including mankind, is one creation and all laws are laws made by the Creator, then there can be no false dualism or dichotomy between the spiritual and the physical. Life is whole and is to be treated as such. Those who trust in medical science alone are just as partial in their view as those who believe only in the miraculous.

Some people have felt deeply impressed to stop taking any medicine and trust God completely. Some of these have had apparently very clear, positive experiences of healing. But it is not a fair generalization to say that we should all therefore follow that course. On the other hand, there are people who went to their doctors or hospitals—never praying at all—who have recovered, too! God not only works directly and miraculously through prayer; he also is at work in all nature and in human intelligence. A person who feels inspired to trust in God alone for miraculous healing should be respected and supported in faith and love by fellow Christians. But that person has no right to make the rules for all.

The old conflict between science and religion is not valid. And it is not fitting for either one to disparage the other. The physician has just about as much right to call attention to some superstitious belief as the clergy has to call attention to blood-letting as a medical practice. We need not "thresh old straw." Let mutual appreciation grow. Let doctor and clergy and counselor and sociologist collaborate for the good of the whole person. Even so, *all* the glory belongs to God.

Wholeness Has Cosmic Meanings

Someone said that the purpose of life is to glorify God and enjoy him forever. There's profound truth in that. The wholeness of right relations with our Creator, with his creation, and with our fellow creatures is life abundant. Jesus Christ is our perfect example in that. He came from God. He lived in uninterrupted fellowship with God. He loved as never any person loved. As C. S. Lewis put it, he was the "grand miracle," the one in whom we find the key to all good things. Being what he was on earth, he had to heal people. He was restoring creation itself.

The Apostle John says, "All things were made by him [Christ, the Word]; and without him was not anything made that was made" (John 1:3). The Apostle Paul said that Christ was "to unite all things in him, things in heaven and things on earth" (Eph. 1:9). Creation comes by him; it is restored by him. How can we help but praise him?

So it is God's will to restore us to wholeness, to harmony with our Creator, the creation, and our fellow creatures. When divine healing is seen in that larger context we know that it has cosmic as well as personal meanings. His will is thus our highest well-being. What a privilege to know him and to be whole!

For Discussion

1. How do you feel about taking medicine? Does it hinder your faith? or is it an aid to faith? Does it keep you from giving the glory to God?

2. Does it increase or decrease your faith to follow the disciplines of balanced diet, exercise, and so forth? How does it make you feel about yourself? Is there any connection between how you feel about yourself and how you exercise faith?

3. Have you ever felt deeply at one with creation, perhaps at a scene of great natural beauty? What does that do to your faith? to your love?

Chapter 12

What If One Is Not Healed?

THE MOST DISTURBING question in relation to healing is why some people are not healed. Let's start out by being perfectly honest. We just don't know! We may surmise. We may speculate. Sometimes we might be cruel enough to add guilt to the illness by insinuating that the person involved has sin in his or her life. But it is hardly appropriate for any of us to "play God" and to come up with "answers" when there is so much within the human psyche and in the human predicament that we do not understand. We cannot chisel away all the questions. If, to believe in healing, we have to provide pat answers, then we are all due for disappointment. It is more fitting that we take off our shoes, for we are on holy ground.

Some Easy "Outs"

What shall we do then? Face up to the mystery and still have faith in God. or take a rationalizing approach avoiding any risk of faith? What if you are prayed for, then you aren't healed? Do you reject the whole idea and become cynical? These are real questions and disturbing thoughts. It will help us to face them openly and candidly.

Some people take refuge in the idea that God sends suffering to bring about spiritual discipline and growth. As we have observed, that was the line of thought accepted for a long time in the Church—the assumption that the body is evil anyhow and probably ought to be punished in order that the soul might prosper. It does seem strange that those who profess to believe this nevertheless try to get well. Perhaps it is pretending to believe something that we haven't thought through which robs us often of realism and true faith in God. Jesus taught that God's will for persons was wholeness, that sickness was an evil oppression. He went about healing people, opening blind eyes—unstopping deaf ears, making the lame to walk, even raising the dead. He would never have tolerated the idea that suffering was sent by God.

Another refuge often taken is in praying, "If it be thy will . . ." Certainly we want to be in God's will. But to pray that way seems to assume that it probably isn't God's will to heal, and the very uncertainty cuts the ground from under our faith. The writer of the Hebrew letter puts the emphasis at the crucial point: "For we have not a high priest who is unable to sympathize with our weaknesses, but one who in every respect has been tempted as we are, yet without sinning. Let us then with confidence draw near to the throne of grace, that we may receive mercy and find grace to help in time of need" (4:15-16). If we are to "come boldly to the throne of grace" we have to believe that it is God's will to make us whole.

A more appropriate attitude, in full awareness of our inadequate understanding, is that of the three Hebrew children when they were threatened with the fiery furnace: "Our God whom we serve is able to deliver us from the burning fiery furnace; and he will deliver us out of your hand, O king. But if not, be it known to you, O king, that we will not serve your gods . . ." (Dan. 3:17-18). "Our God is able to deliver us . . . but if not . . ." we will bow down to nothing less than God!

Why Are Some Not Healed?

We have to parry this question. We are only human and there is so much we don't understand. But we have to try, even though we have to stop short of a complete answer.

Often we hear the inference that there must be sin in the life of that one who is not healed. Now frankly, that might be true in some cases, though we have no right to judge. It is appropriate for the sick person and for all of us to search our own hearts. But it is not right for us to add to the sick one's burden by the assumption that there is something wrong with him or her. The need is for compassion and united faith, not condemnation.

A likely reason, in many cases, is the lack of preparation and instruction. The instruction given in James 5:13 may be a key: "Is any one among you suffering? Let him pray." Does he not refer to the spiritual preparation needed before calling for the elders of the church (v. 14)? Often we have hastened through with the prayer for the sick with little or no preparation, either on the part of the sick one or on the part of the gathered believers. It may be that a fairly extended period of preparation is sometimes needed—dwelling on God's promises, hearing or reading the testimonies of others, for example—in order to develop the attitude of faith.

Most likely the reason why many are not healed is simply that they have not had the united, compassionate prayer support they needed. The sick person often feels very much alone. We must repeat what was said earlier: Prayer for the sick is to be set in the midst of loving, believing friends in Christ. Instead, the responsibility—and sometimes the onus—is often placed fully upon the sick person whose very condition tends to undermine positive attitudes and faith. That's when one most needs the supporting fellowship.

When the disciples questioned Jesus about why they were not successful in the healing of an epileptic boy, he answered that some such cases could be healed only by prayer and fasting (Mark 9:29). It is the experience of many that fasting and prayer bring special spiritual insights and power. It was a fairly common practice in the early church. Is it possible that we are overlooking a great source of power? United prayer and fasting just might be the key to healing in many cases.

Another reason may be that we pray for the specific need alone rather than surrendering ourselves fully to God and receiving the wholeness he offers. For instance, if a hypochondriac comes to be prayed for, the real need is for facing the deeper psychological problem—that of unconsciously wanting to be sick (free of responsibility and being the center of attention as well!). It requires changing the person's basic attitude to life. Counsel is called for, maybe even psychoanalysis. Instead, the act of praying for the sick has been often our unquestioning response to such persons. But it is not a magical formula we have, so that if we go through certain motions we will have certain results. There are conditions to be met and we will have more healings only when we take those conditions more seriously. We need to look for the cause behind the symptoms.

Some are not healed—or if they are healed they soon are back as they were before—because the basic attitudes and habits have not been changed. What if God healed everybody right now? The gluttons would go on eating too much, the alcoholics would continue to destroy themselves, the worriers would develop new stomach ulcers, and so on. Many a victory has been lost by a lack of discipline in attitudes and a return to the causes of illness.

There may be other plausible reasons why some people are not healed, but not all sufferers are to be placed in such categories. We can't explain away all cases. We simply try to understand as much as we can, then stand bareheaded before the remaining mystery. Let the healing specialists make their sweeping claims (they don't tell us about the ones who are not healed!)—we have to recognize our limitations and we have to be scrupulously honest about "results."

Probably the greatest reason of all for the limited amount of healing that takes place among us is *the lack of faith*. The general spiritual tone of any congregation tends to decline unless there is strong teaching and leadership. We live with relatively little sense of real need. We depend so much on science and human resources; the result is that we neglect our highest spiritual privileges. About the only time we get in real earnest is when all the human resources run out; then we are hardly prepared spiritually to exercise real faith.

What If You Are Not Healed?

We are affirming God's will for our healing and wholeness. We are also recognizing that we simply do not understand the human psyche and the human predicament. With the enigma now before us we must ask: If you are not healed, how do you handle the problem within yourself? You can sink into the quicksand of self-pity, but that will only add to your burden, and it will make you a burden. You can stew in the juices of resentment but you will only "cook your own goose."

Among the noblest, most radiant and courageous people some of us ever have known have been people who have suffered much and have borne their burden with continuing faith. One is tempted to agree with the idea that God sent the suffering, but that would be untenable as a conclusion. We can, however, affirm that God's grace is sufficient. We can attest the truth of that great promise that "in everything God works for good with those who love him" (Rom. 8:28). Suffering can indeed be an experience in growth and maturity.

This apparently was true of the Apostle Paul. He spoke of some experiences so sacred to him that he spoke in the third person in his description. Then he added, "And to keep me from being too elated by the abundance of revelations, a thorn was given me in the flesh . . ." That would seem to say that God gave him the "thorn," but he added the explanation, "a messenger of Satan, to harass me, to keep me

97

from being too elated." He saw his affliction, whatever it was, as coming from Satan, though perhaps permitted by God as was true in the case of Job. In any case, he said, "Three times I besought the Lord about this, that it should leave me; but he said to me, 'My grace is sufficient for you, for my power is made perfect in weakness" (2 Cor. 12:7-9). Paul apparently felt that he needed the humbling, mellowing effect of his "thorn." He felt it came from Satan, not from God. He found the grace of God sufficient. Valuable lessons indeed!

One great genius of Christianity is its overcoming of evil by good. Jesus did just that in his crucifixion. The cross, always a symbol of ignominy and shame, was transformed into the symbol of hope. Love overcame hate. Righteousness triumphed over evil. Paul was true to this principle when he enjoined the Roman Christians to "overcome evil with good."

We need not say that God sends affliction in order to affirm that God can work out a larger purpose in spite of—or perhaps through— such affliction. Jesus did not see the cross as something from God. He saw it as the product and instrument of evil. But he bore it in the full demonstration of God's love. It is important that we see this distinction in connection with affliction and healing.

One of Satan's favorite tricks is to get us doubting ourselves. He whispers, "If you were a real Christian, and if you had real faith, this affliction would never have come upon you." Remember that was the tactic Satan used in testing Jesus. "If you are the Son of God, make these stones bread." (Matt. 4:3). It was intended to create doubt in his mind. But Jesus knew who he was. He had no need for some confirming "evidence" to satisfy the enemy. Perhaps the most devastating thing in affliction for most people is the self-condemnation, the debilitating doubt. Those who rise above the confusion are the ones who are sure of God's love and grace, those who can see that God is working out his purpose even in the midst of our weaknesses and our human predicament.

Much can be learned in time of affliction, perhaps chiefly what we are lacking in solid spiritual foundations. Whereas we have concentrated on work and relied on personal strength, we now are thrown back upon inner resources. Whereas once we felt independent and self-sufficient, we now feel a common bond and solidarity with others in elemental needs. Many people have found, in time of affliction, a new foundation for their lives and a new purpose for living. Thus the experience may actually be a healing one at deeper levels. We may think through many things previously neglected, growing intellectually and maturing emotionally. Affliction is not sent by God, but by the grace of God we can use it for significant self-discovery and spiritual growth.

The Ultimate Healing

How many times we have said of a deceased loved one, "He won't have to suffer any more!" Death comes as the perfect rest and perfect healing. For the believing Christian death has lost its "sting" and the grave its "victory." The Apostle wrote to the Corinthian believers: "He [Christ] must reign until he has put all his enemies under his feet. The last enemy to be destroyed is death" (1 Cor. 15:25-26). So long as we are part of the human existence and the frailties of the flesh we will be subject to certain limitations. But the full and perfect deliverance awaits us. Graduation time comes. Then we can say, like Paul, "I have finished my course . . ."

For Discussion

1. How many people do you know who were prayed for and healed? How many were not healed? Try to explain this. Were those who were healed "better" Christians?

2. In what sense do we doubt ourselves when we need healing? What causes uncertainty? Is it really doubting God that bothers us, or is it doubting ourselves? Is it our sense of unworthiness?

3. How do you really feel about our concern for one another in time of sickness? How well do we "bear one another's burdens"? How can we improve our mutual care?

4. Can we look upon death as release, as ultimate healing? or is this a cop-out?

Personal Notes

Chapter 13

Fostering a Healing Ministry

EVEN a cursory reading of the New Testament will convince us that probably the most important single factor in the success of early Christianity was the *miraculous* element which characterized it. In the ministry of Jesus, healings and miracles of various kinds catapulted him into immediate fame across that small country. After the three great tests in the wilderness, he apparently performed a good many miracles even before going to the Nazareth synagogue where he read from the prophet Isaiah (Chapter 61) the commission he had accepted as his own. For about three years, he had crowds pressing in on him wherever he went. One very significant reason for that was the desire on the part of so many people to be healed.

This also was true in the early church. Those early Christians could not be ignored. There were too many unusual experiences which attended their lives and worship. They lived among miracles. They were persecuted but they couldn't be written off. The account in Acts says that of the outsiders none dared join themselves to them but the people magnified them.

It is true today. Wherever there are miracles, people go. Where they find help they go. Many congregations are ignored simply because nothing is happening there. However beautiful the worship, however eloquent the sermon, people still respond best when their needs are identified and met.

What Hinders Our Faith?

As mentioned before, the overwhelming influence of science and medicine seems to make faith less necessary. The typical mode of reasoning now is *inductive*—from particulars to a general conclusion. The mode of reasoning in the Christian faith is *deductive*—from the general proposition or revealed truth to the particular application. In this sense we are a bit out of gear with our times. Therefore, we have to demonstrate the efficacy of what we believe. People may be skeptical (even Christian people absorb this attitude), but they pay attention when the power of God is demonstrated.

Curiously enough, another hindrance to faith may be the sweeping claims made by a few for divine healing. Many non-Christian people back away from that, and some Christian people feel uneasy. For one thing, there are too many inconsistencies in those claims. There is sometimes a lack of integrity and the whole thing comes off as partially false. The "healer" can "fold his tent like an Arab and silently steal away"—but sincere, credulous people have to live with the disillusionment.

It would seem, then, that lasting faith will be most encouraged by scrupulous honesty and realism about healing. In our keen desire for healing we are often credulous and vulnerable to extravagant claims. Responsible teaching is necessary to foster true and sustained faith for healing.

Recover Biblical Holism

Faith is inspired by the holistic view of creation and life which we see in the Bible. Let's say it again: All of creation is under God's lordship and control. He gave us our bodies as well as our minds and souls. His will is our wholeness. When we have that view of life our faith is increased. If, on the other hand, we view our bodies as something dirty and contemptible, it is difficult to believe in healing as God's will. The framework of our thinking is important to our faith. We have made quite a point of this just because there is so much wrong thinking and because the proper, biblical view is essential to the joyous life of positive faith. It is remarkable how much self-contempt passes for humility and how much rejection of God's good creation passes for resignation to the will of God. If God wills our wholeness, then submission to his will is the way of positive faith. The coming of Jesus Christ was the influx of sheer joy and peace because Jesus was saying, "Look, God loves you. He wants to make you whole." And Jesus' whole ministry was one of making people whole.

The holistic view also relieves our minds of that supposed conflict between the spiritual and the physical. To suppose that the knowledge of physical laws and the attempt to live in harmony with the physical universe is a denial of faith is a false supposition which sets up conflict within ourselves. We can't make sense of it all. The holistic view relieves us of the confusion and enables us to rejoice in our entire being.

This is not by any means to overlook the reality of evil or its devastating effects. It is simply to say that the physical, per se, is not evil. There are the physical drives which can be, and often are, expressed in evil ways. But yielded to God, our very bodies and minds may be "instruments of righteousness" and a "living sacrifice holy and acceptable unto God." Faith is inspired by this holistic view of life and creation.

Positive Scriptural Teaching

"Faith cometh by hearing, and hearing by the Word of God" says Romans 10:17. "Faith is awakened by the message . . ." (NEB). Wherever there is consistent, responsible teaching of the Scripture, faith will be found increasingly strong. This is more than crying, "Have faith." Faith is not something subjective we "psych" ourselves into and thus produce some result. It is *the steady view of God* as revealed in the Scriptures. It does not arise within us. It is in the fact that God himself has taken the initiative and acted on our behalf, and in the fact of our response to his mighty acts. We speak not of faith in faith, but of faith in God.

The view expressed in 2 Peter 1:3-4 is the key: "His divine power has granted to us all things that pertain to life and godliness, through the knowledge of him who called us to his own glory and excellence, by which he has granted to us his precious and very great promises, that through these you may escape from the corruption that is in the world because of passion, and become partakers of the divine nature." God reveals his divine power, providing to us all things necessary, giving us his great promises. Through these promises one becomes a partaker of the divine nature. Daring thought! But a promise involves the giving of oneself in pledge and commitment. To believe and count on the promise given is to receive something of the nature and character of the one making the promise. It is life-sharing in nature.

This is why positive faith is inspired by positive scriptural teaching. Teaching on the ethical implications of current events and on psychological principles that may help us understand ourselves may be good, but they are not particularly faith inspiring. The exposition of Scripture is. Especially is this true when the great promises are stressed. Faith is not a vague state of mind. It is not some sort of intangible entity you get. It is believing God's promises. And to hear those promises, to give them sustained attention, inspires belief.

Teach Wholeness of Life

If God is Creator and Lord of all life, if he loves us with an unconditional love, and if he gives himself to us in great promises, then our response to him ought to be a total response—physically, intellectually, spiritually. Our seeking for healing ought to be seeking for wholeness. It ought to be seeking his lordship in our whole lives, not seeking to use him for the healing of some particular malady while withholding ourselves from him. As we have observed before, the forgiveness of sins and the healing of body and mind go together. The human being is one being.

Many of our Christian privileges are neglected or ignored because we have thought in a fragmented manner, as though God was interested only in our souls. "All things are yours . . . and you are Christ's; and Christ is God's" (1 Cor. 3:21,23) wrote Paul. He was saying that we do not have to settle for fragments. While he was not referring directly to healing in that passage, the principle holds true.

Develop the Caring Fellowship

Individuals should not stand alone in time of need. They are part, normally, of the Body of Christ, the fellowship of believers. This also is a part of the wholeness. We belong together. We need one another. Our Lord Jesus promised to meet with us when we come together in his name. It is in the caring fellowship where we have our finest experiences of healing.

But this quality of fellowship doesn't just happen. It is developed by positive teaching and example. It is fostered by openness to one another, by listening lovingly, by sharing burdens, by expressing confidence and appreciation. (That congregation where the critical, judgmental spirit abounds will have few experiences of healing.) It is renewed by the removal of unseen barriers like prejudice, suspicion, grudges, and unresolved guilt. The fellowship is *always* in need of renewal. It is like the human body which constantly rids itself of waste and poisons while at the same time receiving food and nourishment, building new cells, and renewing itself. Ephesians 4:15-16 tells us that "we are to grow up in every way into him who is the head, into Christ, from whom the whole body, joined and knit together by every joint with which it is supplied, when each part is working properly, makes bodily growth and upbuilds itself in love." That is to say, the body of believers has within it the genius of renewal and growth because of the presence of Christ within it. And healing is set in this context of mutual ministry.

Recognize the Gifts of the Spirit

According to the list of gifts of the Holy Spirit given in 1 Corinthians 12:9-10 there are, among the others, the gift of "faith," the "gifts of healing," and "the working of miracles." Note that in relation to healing the plural is used— "*gifts* of healing." It may be that the Apostle recognized different kinds of healing or different kinds of maladies in which some sensitivity of discernment and understanding was indicated. In any case, these gifts of the Spirit would seem to be closely related—the gift of faith, the gifts of healing, and the gift of miracles. One translation says "miraculous powers."

Clearly some of the early Christians were powerfully used of God in performing miracles among them. It has been true in greater or lesser degree through the history of the Church. Some of those so gifted have become widely known. Others have been less conspicuous but have nevertheless been instrumental in bringing healing.

One thing the Apostle stresses is the fact that all gifts of the Spirit are given to the Church, and they are to be exercised as part of the Church's ministry. "To each is given the manifestation of the Spirit for the common good" (1 Cor. 12:7). There are "varieties of gifts, but the same Spirit; and there are varieties of service, but the same Lord; and there are varieties of working, but it is the same God who inspires them all in every one" (vv 4-6). There is corporateness and solidarity here. "There is one body and one Spirit . . . one Lord, one faith, one baptism, one God and Father of us all, who is above all and through all and in all" (Eph 4:4-6). It is in that context that the Apostle says, in the next verse, that "grace was given to each of us according to the measure of Christ's gift."

It is important that we recognize the gifting of the Holy Spirit and not allow the spirit of rivalry or cynicism or criticism ever to rob us of the full ministry of the Spirit. We cannot honor the Spirit without recognizing his gifts. They should be encouraged. We ought to pray that God will raise up among us the ones he chooses for special ministries, and we ought always to be seeking God's will for every person's life.

Let us take whatever steps are necessary and meet whatever conditions we must to restore fully the healing ministry of the Church and the full operation of the Holy Spirit. Let us never surrender the wonderful ministry of healing to the entrepreneur or the charlatan. The healing ministry is to be a normal part of the Church's life. It is there, in the loving, caring fellowship, that it ought most to take place—where preparation and counsel can be provided, where the undergirding faith of Christian friends is present, where continuing support and encouragement can be offered, where healing and wholeness is experienced.

For Discussion

1. How do you feel about the level of faith among us? Is faith increasing or decreasing? What can we do to increase our own faith and encourage the faith of others?

2. Much has been made in this book of three points: (1) the holistic view of life as taught in the Bible, (2) the need to be aware of all God's laws as taught in the Bible and the need to live within them, and (3) the great importance of the caring fellowship in trusting God together. Now how do you react to that frame of reasoning? Does it encourage or discourage your faith?

3. In our fellowship we always have taught and practiced healing. Once that teaching was quite different from others. Now it is much more commonly accepted. What course should we take from here?

Personal Notes

Personal Notes

Personal Notes